The Sciences Po Series in International Relations and Political Economy

Series Editor
Alain Dieckhoff, Center for International Studies (CERI),
Sciences Po - CNRS, Paris, France

Advisory Editor
Miriam Perier, Center for International Studies (CERI),
Sciences Po - CNRS, Paris, France

The Sciences Po Series in International Relations and Political Economy focuses on the transformations of the international arena and of political societies, in a world where the state keeps reinventing itself and appears resilient in many ways, though its sovereignty is increasingly questioned. The series publishes books that have two main objectives: explore the various aspects of contemporary international/transnational relations, from a theoretical and an empirical perspective; and analyze the transformations of political societies through comparative lenses. Evolution in world affairs sustains a variety of networks from the ideological to the criminal or terrorist that impact both on international relations and local societies. Besides the geopolitical transformations of the globalized planet, the new political economy of the world has a decided impact on its destiny as well, and this series hopes to uncover what that is.

The series consists of works emanating from the foremost French researchers from Sciences Po, Paris. It also welcomes works by academics who share our methods and philosophy of research in an open-minded perspective of what academic research in social sciences allows for and should aim for. Sciences Po was founded in 1872 and is today one of the most prestigious universities for teaching and research in social sciences in France, recognized worldwide.

Mohamed-Ali Adraoui

Understanding Salafism

Mohamed-Ali Adraoui
Center for International Studies
Sciences Po
Paris, France

ISSN 2945-607X   ISSN 2945-6088 (electronic)
The Sciences Po Series in International Relations and Political Economy
ISBN 978-3-031-18088-0   ISBN 978-3-031-18089-7 (eBook)
https://doi.org/10.1007/978-3-031-18089-7

© The Author(s), under exclusive license to Springer Nature Switzerland AG 2022
This work is subject to copyright. All rights are solely and exclusively licensed by the Publisher, whether the whole or part of the material is concerned, specifically the rights of translation, reprinting, reuse of illustrations, recitation, broadcasting, reproduction on microfilms or in any other physical way, and transmission or information storage and retrieval, electronic adaptation, computer software, or by similar or dissimilar methodology now known or hereafter developed.
The use of general descriptive names, registered names, trademarks, service marks, etc. in this publication does not imply, even in the absence of a specific statement, that such names are exempt from the relevant protective laws and regulations and therefore free for general use.
The publisher, the authors, and the editors are safe to assume that the advice and information in this book are believed to be true and accurate at the date of publication. Neither the publisher nor the authors or the editors give a warranty, expressed or implied, with respect to the material contained herein or for any errors or omissions that may have been made. The publisher remains neutral with regard to jurisdictional claims in published maps and institutional affiliations.

Cover illustration: © MirageC gettyimages

This Palgrave Macmillan imprint is published by the registered company Springer Nature Switzerland AG
The registered company address is: Gewerbestrasse 11, 6330 Cham, Switzerland

Acknowledgments

I have conceived the present book as a necessary step in my attempt to understand and interpret the debates and developments characterizing contemporary Salafism. For nearly twenty years, I have been working with a brilliant generation of scholars on every continent of the world to study what this vision of Islam, which claims to restore the discourses, practices, and symbols supposedly abandoned by the majority of Muslims in the world, might be echoing.

By means of a resolutely multidisciplinary approach, I have thus tried in a few words and within the framework of a collection in which I have the honor of publishing this modest work, to shed light on the main theoretical and empirical issues allowing us to understand Salafism.

My warm and sincere thanks go to my parents, Ahmed and Khadija Adraoui, as well as to the director of the international research center of Sciences Po, Alain Dieckhoff, who allowed the publication of this book which will bring, I hope, some keys of comprehension to a politico-religious phenomenon counting among the most debated of our time. I would also like to express my gratitude to Miriam Perier for all her efforts and encouragement since the first time it was proposed to publish this book in the excellent collection dedicated to Sciences Po Paris at Palgrave.

I would also like to thank all my colleagues, in so many countries, for their invaluable proofreading and pointed remarks on the main ideas and examples highlighted in this work. I am also grateful to my colleagues

Francesco Cavatorta and Jonathan Brown for reading and encouraging the reading of this work.

Finally, I would like to thank the readers for agreeing to travel for a few pages in the world of Salafism.

Praise for *Understanding Salafism*

"This book offers concise, one-stop shopping for anyone interested in the complicated history, debates and contemporary political roots and ramifications of Salafism, a school of thought and contested movement in the Muslim world with consistently crucial consequences."
—Jonathan AC Brown, *School of Foreign Service, Georgetown University, US*

"Adraoui's book is a welcome contribution to the literature on the much misunderstood phenomenon of Salafism in the contemporary age. It is a must-read for all those who want to beging exploring its meaning, characteristics and reach."
—Francesco Cavatorta, *professor of political science at Universite Laval in Quebec, Canada*

Contents

1	Understanding Salafism: A Few Introductory Remarks	1
2	Defining Salafism: What Is at Stake?	5
	Salafism: An Attempt at a Definition	5
	Understanding Salafism: The Need to Reflect in Terms of Mental Topography	8
	References	10
3	Salafism: A Brief History	11
	References	15
4	The Basics of the Salafist Ethic	17
	The Cleric, or the Cornerstone of the Salafist Meaning System	17
	Literalism or Scripturalism?	20
	Reference	22
5	The Globalization of Salafism	23
	The Statization of Salafism with the Birth and the Rise of Modern Saudi Arabia	24
	The Saudization of Salafism in the Twentieth Century: When Saudi Arabia Speaks for Islam and the Umma	27
	A Two-Level State Salafism: Clerics and Kings	28
	Reference	30

6	**The Fragmentation and Crisis of Salafism: The Saudi Turn and the Rise of New Ideological Contenders**	31
	From Consensus to Crisis of Legitimacy: The Fragmentation and Explosion of the Global Salafist Field Around the Question of the Sa'ud. The Challenge of Islamism, Jihadism, and Democratization	31
	From an Offensive Salafism to a Defensive Form of Salafism	31
	The Emergence of Salafism-Jihadism and the Crisis of Saudi Religious and Political Legitimacy	34
	Since the Arab Revolutions: Saudi Arabia Between Positive and Negative Centrality	36
	The Rise of a "Soft Salafism": Religious Reformation in Saudi Arabia?	38
	References	39
7	**Salafism and Modernity: Beyond Politics**	41
	Crisis of Traditional Authority and Divorce Between Culture and Religion	41
	Islam of Globalization? When Fundamentalism is Modern	44
	The Salafist Economic Ethics: Salvation by Worldly Success?	45
	Salafism and Migration: The Case of Hijra	46
	The Hijra in Salafism: The Fulfillment of "Allegiance and Disavowal"	47
	The Internal Hijra: *Between Symbolic Withdrawal and the Premises of Departure*	48
	The Short-Term Hijra: *A First Step Toward a Final Break*	51
	The Final Hijra: *Completion of the Rupture?*	52
	References	55
8	**Understanding Past and Today Jihadism**	57
	From Jihād *to Jihadism*	57
	Armed Jihād *Between Historical Exception and Today Systematization*	57
	The Contemporary Origins of Jihadism	59
	The Core Questions in Jihadism	61
	Who is the Enemy?	61
	Who Must Lead Jihād *and Jihadism?*	68
	The Role of Jihadist Endeavor in the Definition of Being a Muslim	70

	How to Strategize and Lead Jihadism Militarily?	72
	Joining a Foreign Jihadist Movement.	73
	Terrorist Radicalization	74
	References	78
9	**Salafism in Context: Understanding the Issue of Ideological and Social Permeability, and the Value Placed on Quietism, Political Participation and Violence**	81
	Salafism and Violence: Is Political Change Desirable? if Yes, How to Achieve It?	82
	Beyond the Fragmentation of Salafism: Is Jihadism Getting Autonomized?	85
	Salafism and Jihadism: A Common Doctrinal Heritage	87
	Jihadist Differentiation from Salafism	89
	Empowerment of Jihadism: Violence Without Religious Socialization	90
	Apocalypticism of Islamic State Jihadism	92
	Post-Islamic State Jihadism	93
	References	96
10	**By Way of Conclusion: Salafism, a Container More Than a Content? Beyond the Essentialization of a Fundamentalism**	97
References		**101**

CHAPTER 1

Understanding Salafism: A Few Introductory Remarks

Abstract This chapter highlights the need to study Salafism in a dispassionate manner, mobilizing a multidisciplinary approach and asking the key questions through which such a vision of Islam has been and continues to be successful, in different (sometimes opposing) forms, within various social, cultural, and historical contexts.

Keyword A timely book

There are few terms today that provoke so much fear. Politicians,[1] journalists, activists, intellectuals, and "simple" citizens have been intrigued by Salafism for several years, by its dress code, puritan language, fundamentalist imaginary, transnational connections, and its potential role in explaining violent extremist movements (often referred to as Jihadist). A

---

[1] "*Manuel Valls: le salafisme est en train de gagner la bataille de l'islam de France*", *Le Figaro*, April 5, 2016. The former French prime minister declaring, several months before the presidential election of 2017, that this struggle would be above all else a "cultural and identity battle" during a conference organized in Paris dealing with "radical Islamism and the political distortion in Europe," after having taken care to insist on the fact that one "active minority (represented by) Salafist groups (were) winning the ideological and cultural battle" of Islam in France.

© The Author(s), under exclusive license to Springer Nature Switzerland AG 2022
M.-A. Adraoui, *Understanding Salafism*, The Sciences Po Series in International Relations and Political Economy,
https://doi.org/10.1007/978-3-031-18089-7_1

number of questions about security, law, society, diplomacy, or (private and public) morality have indeed emerged in the wake of this branch of Islam *(Islām)*, which can be considered new given its recent appearance within a number of societies, but also ancient and even original if we believe Salafist devotees. Claiming to follow in the footsteps of the *salaf ṣāliḥ*, paradigmatic figures of *sunnī* Islam for being contemporary proponents of the Prophet Muḥammad, the physical and moral incarnation of authentic Islamic virtues, Salafists explicitly embody in this respect a religious revivalism. This latter enjoys a certain success both in historical Islamic territories and in predominately non-Muslim contexts such as the United States, Sweden, France, Nigeria, Azerbaijan, or Cambodia.

Understanding Salafism requires thinking along several dimensions. Whether one is interested in the trajectory of an individual who embraces Salafist canonical principles and attitudes, the international political context that has favored the globalization of Salafism for several decades, or even the long history of events and evolutions during which an *episteme*[2] rooted in "orthodoxy" and "orthopraxy" was developed, it is necessary to grasp numerous dimensions coming from a number of actors within diverse social-cultural contexts. Another singularity linked to this theme, once a definition of this concept is attempted as we will see below, is related to the diversity of conceptions and practices of Salafism as well as the relationships of competition opposing various protagonists in this "return to/restore the roots" dynamic. Is it indeed legitimate to claim to want to understand Salafism? How can we pinpoint the fundamental desire to go back in history in order to reintroduce the past in the present in anticipation of the future? Is it appropriate to see this as an above all political ideology, born out of a desire to recover the course of history during an unfavorable time for Muslims? Or is Salafism first and foremost, as consciously fundamentalist as it is, a reformist movement whose aim is primarily to re-establish the rights of a supposedly neglected dogma? Considering the nature of Salafism as the fruit of an encounter between an (individual or collective) imaginary and a specific historical situation proves to be a pertinent way to reason in that this allows a certain subjectivity to be accounted for while shedding light on the conditions in which this revivalist ethics has developed, and hence on the explanatory factors of the diversity and likely course of Salafism. While

---

[2] See below.

it is essential to focus on the religious meanings of the identification with the very first generations of Muslims, it is equally important to historicize the forms of engagement related to this doctrinal construction so as to assess the complexity of fundamentalism in the contemporary era as well as the intricacy of multiple considerations (social, political, psychological, anthropological, etc.) without which it is impossible to know what Salafism actually means.

This modest contribution draws on over fifteen years of research on puritan experiment that has been undeniably successful within a number of diverse fields, whether in geographical, ideological, political, social, cultural, and of course, religious terms,[3] in short chapters without (at least I hope) compromising on the necessary scientific rigor. Studies of Salafism, or ones that more generally address forms of revivalism and fundamentalist engagement within contemporary Islam, have experienced a considerable boom given significant current events, making it more than ever necessary for scholars to provide understanding to a wide audience that is rightfully keen on gaining knowledge based on true fieldwork far from the urgency of the media. In a time where some seem to doubt of the pertinence or usefulness of history and social sciences, through this short book I demonstrate (if it was still needed) that a proper knowledge of dynamics having an impact on our societies for several years to come can only be done from a healthy distance, far from the immediate political or partisan rationales. Trying to understand Salafism requires putting into temporal perspective a great number of phenomena and events possibly having at the end of the day little to do with many of the current discourses surrounding the interpretation of this fundamentalist narrative—thus making it necessary to bring together several questions in the aim of providing greater understanding to the ongoing debate on this religious branch.

---

[3] Which in and of itself deserves specific attention since the visibility of a such a fundamentalist form within different contexts is too charged with meaning to be ignored.

CHAPTER 2

Defining Salafism: What Is at Stake?

Abstract This section offers an etymological and symbolic definition of the vision of Islam and history to which the Salafists refer. The chapter allows us to understand why it is legitimate to see in this religious current a fundamentalist and puritanical form of the Muslim religion.

Keywords Tawhid · Salaf Salih · Fundamentalism · Integralism · Radicalism · Intransigeantism

SALAFISM: AN ATTEMPT AT A DEFINITION

In the Muslim faith, Muḥammad (571–632), by his apostolate, revealed a belief system to the world, delivered a message, and, by doing so, sealed the Prophecy (which had begun with the first man and Messenger, Adam). If authenticity is represented in the man (in his deeds, words, and acquiescence which contribute to forming the *sunna*[1]), it did not dissolve after the disappearance of Muḥammad, since his contemporaries as well

---

[1] The path of Muḥammad, source of truth and exemplariness after the *Qurʾān* which features the Word of God uncreated in *sunnī* Islam. *Shīʿa* Islam adopts another understanding which is centered on the belief that the Truth is transmitted first within the

© The Author(s), under exclusive license to Springer Nature Switzerland AG 2022
M.-A. Adraoui, *Understanding Salafism*, The Sciences Po Series in International Relations and Political Economy,
https://doi.org/10.1007/978-3-031-18089-7_2

as successive generations[2] remain steeped in his paragon. While a multitude of ways of apprehending and understanding Islam have emerged since its beginnings, only one is supposed to have remained faithful to Muhammad's call according to the Salafists. Claiming in both the proper sense and figurative sense of the word an ethics of rectitude and restoration, Salafists, meaning those who seek to follow in the footsteps of the *salaf al-ṣāliḥ*, see themselves as remaining scrupulously on the path that leads from the present to the origins. Among other possible ways, their existence and morality are founded on a specific and exclusive *minhāj* ("path"), that of the Ancient Sages (or Pious Predecessors, or Virtuous Ancestors, or Righteous Precursors).

Each word in Arabic comes from a root (contributing to the meaning of the term) onto which is added a scheme (which determines the grammatical nature of the word used). *Salaf* thus comes from the root s-l-f which echoes back to anteriority and precedence. Unlike kh-l-f, which refers to succession and consecutiveness,[3] this root has the main function of illustrating a search for the origin. The latter represents the only true condition of authenticity in that time which passes is supposed to have brought deviationism in opposition to "the straight path" that Salafists intend to revive. The second word *ṣāliḥ* comes from the root ṣ-l-ḥ which is that of value and virtue. Giving rise, for instance, to the first name *Salāḥ*,[4] it particularly describes piousness in the religious sphere and morality. Thus referring to the first Muslims as the paradigmatic models of faith and practice, Salafists have erected the early times of Islam as the only period of history whose characteristics must be strictly reproduced. Representing

---

family of Muḥammad, and specifically among his descendants, making up the imams that will transmit this privileged relationship with the Truth from one generation to another.

[2] At the basis of Salafist reasoning, there is reference to a word of Muḥammad addressing the relative value of different eras of history which sheds light on the exemplary piousness of the first three generations/eras of Muslims thus established as models of virtue: "The best people are my contemporaries, and then those who will follow them, then those who will follow them." *Collection of Authentic Prophetic Words*, imam Bukhārī, *hadīth* number 6248.

[3] The term *khalif* is based on this root. It refers in the history of Muslim societies to the title used by Muḥammad's successors, the Caliph being the successor of the Messenger of God.

[4] The *Sulṭān* and the conqueror of Jerusalem (*al-Quds*), Salāḥ al-dīn al-Ayyūbī (Saladin, 1138–1193) winner of the Battle of Ḥaṭṭīn in 1187, is a famous example of this.

in a substantial way a paradigm (which the followers present as "scientific" since it is based on a rigorous scholarly approach), preaching (since it is a call to return to "the right path") and a state of authenticity (in that it provides an exclusive "genuine" moral, religious, and social content), Salafism is thus the form of Islam that is supposed to contain the highest level of purity, and which must see itself as a revivalist and restorationist thought.

Over the centuries, and notably through the intervention of clerics who wanted to call their co-religionists to order, puritan reforms focusing on the need to return to the teachings of the *salaf* have emerged. One of the most famous is undoubtedly that initiated in the Arabian Peninsula in the eighteenth century. If today the term "wahhabism" is often lumped together with that of Salafism, it is essentially because in this geographic location at that time, an imam and preacher named Muḥammad b. Abd al-Wahhāb (1703–1792) was seeking, in a context that he thought had become religiously heterodox, to re-establish the rights of a dogma *(al-ʿaqīda)* that he considered had been trampled on (Al-Rasheed 2010; Commins 2006). He thus vilified and fought the wrong practices that had become usual at the time according to him, namely the worship of graves when neither intercession (asking another to pray to God for oneself, direct prayers being permitted) nor veneration of another besides Him are supposed to be part of the Ancients' faith and can in certain cases lead to anathema. However, his main political success is undoubtedly to have turned his puritan preaching in a more political direction by forming an alliance throughout his life with Muḥammad b. Saʿūd (1687–1765), a tribal leader from the *Najd* region who wanted to spread his power by giving him a religious anointing from the cleric hoping to give more strength to his fundamentalist reform. This alliance, which took the form of a pact dating from 1744 in the name of which Muḥammad b. Saʿūd supported the preaching of what would become the religious reference of the young state. In exchange for his support, his duty was to govern in compliance with b. Abd al-Wahhāb's advice and to defend the principle of divine unicity (*al-tawḥīd*) threatened by "the deviations" of that time. This pact lies at the origin of the first Saudi kingdom whose role will be highlighted later on across this book. The latter served as a model for other alliances based on this complicit transaction (Mouline 2014) between tribal leaders and clerics, thus illustrating a difference of roles and authorities in Muslim land but also a founding collusion when religious scholars and rulers decide to collaborate on a project combining puritan reform, state-building, and territorial conquest. Although defeated by its neighbors in the end, this first Saudi state comes back to life on several occasions, particularly between the two world wars with the new conquest of *Ḥijāz* after 1926 and the unification of the kingdom in 1932, at the instigation of a descendant of Muḥammad b. Sa'ud ('Abd al-'Azīz b. Sa'ūd, 1876–1953), once again supported by the descendants of Muḥammad b. Abd al-Wahhāb (forming the al-Shaykh family which still represents today the religious backbone of the Saudi state and monarchy requested by these religious authorities to export Salafism on a worldwide scale as would be the case in the twentieth century).

Understanding Salafism: The Need to Reflect in Terms of Mental Topography

"Laysa hadhā min al-salaf!". "This is not the way of the Salaf!". Using these Arabic words, a young Salafist imam from a mosque in Montreuil, near Paris, a few years ago warned his followers against certain behaviors that he deemed contrary to the faith of the Ancients. By referring to a generation of believers whose trace (*al-athar*) left in history must consequently serve as a model of morality and behavior for Muslims, the young cleric and preacher (*al-dā'ī*) is, in doing so, the protagonist of a key scene in the Salafist imaginary. Illustrating the mission of calling to order which belongs to the person invested in the study of Islamic scriptures (above all the *Qur'ān* and the *sunna* of the Prophet Muḥammad), this example moreover echoes the heart of the revivalist approach specific to Salafism.

Understanding Salafism requires above all other considerations grasping the procedure of mental topography that has defined this original form of religious preaching for several centuries. Echoing a cyclical logic according to which human beings should remain distinguished by a state of permanence notwithstanding the social, cultural, and political configurations of which they are a part, history must be animated, whatever the versions of Salafism we focus on, by the same epistemic motivation. It is, more specifically, a double movement, as if the individual trajectory and the collective destiny of a society needed to follow the same injunctions. Renewing with a past that is synonymous with authenticity is the only way to be regenerated in the present moment and to rediscover what is supposed to represent its essence in order to project oneself to their advantage into the future. This double animation is based on the interpretation of life and morality in topographical terms.

Islam is presented as one, at the very least in terms of "true" content. Muḥammad, by his apostolate, revealed the last only religion to be accepted by human beings. From then on, his contemporaries as well as successive generations are to remain impregnated with his model. While a number of ways of apprehending and understanding Islam emerged since the beginning, only one is said to have remained faithful to the call of Muḥammad. Claiming to be an ethics of rectitude in both the literal and figurative sense of the term, Salafists, meaning those who follow in the footsteps of the *salaf ṣāliḥ*, see themselves as having scrupulously remained on the path that leads from the origin to the present era. Referring thus to the first Muslims as the paradigmatic models of faith and practice, Salafists have thus built up the early times of Islam as the Golden Era, the features of which must be reproduced. If Islam is gold, other versions of this religion have, in the eyes of Salafists, lost purity over the centuries, at the risk of no longer being able to claim to be called "golden."

This is the second dimension of the mental topography defining Salafism (*al-salafiyya*) that can be grasped as a reform movement that is fundamentalist (in the first sense of the word since it is a question of returning to the fundamental concept of Islam) and puritan (the deviance attributed to other branches not having yet done its work when religion was in the hands of those having assimilated it from the Prophet himself). Returning to the Salafists is not enough if this process is not accompanied by a new socialization whose purpose is to defend and spread the path of the Pious Predecessors today. In this respect, it is a question of a new path to trace in the name of the religious imperative defining Salafist revivalism. If this puts their tenants in opposition with the contemporary norm (de facto illegitimate if it contradicts that which prevailed in the original era), then the separation becomes not only permitted but desirable since the capital of purity accumulated in the eyes of Salafists risks corruption (potentially announcing perdition in the afterlife).[5] This double view

---

[5] In this respect, Salafism is a form of radical integralism (Donegani 1993) and intransigentism (Poulat 1986). The "uncompromising" Salafist approach is similar to the intransigent attitude of French Catholics in late nineteenth century as explained by Émile Poulat. For him, the "intransigent Catholics" were those who were totally loyal to the Church's teachings and commands and hence refused to make any concession to modern ideas that questioned the fundamentals of their faith. The Salafists today are very loyal to what regard as authentic, unsurpassable Islamic origins and refuse any element they deem exogenous to this initial universe of Islam. In like manner, Jean-Marie Donegani talks about "integralist-radical Catholics" of France who were highly critical to the clear

(first toward the past and then toward the future) is at the basis of the socialization promoted by Salafists. The latter can make us think (despite many differences) of the experience of born-again Christians for which a form of renaissance presides over a new existence based on the respect of biblical principles. By becoming re-affiliated genealogically with the first generations of Muslims, and then with all believers having claimed to (re)live their heritage across centuries, a symbolic straight line is supposed to link contemporary Salafists to the first historical Muslims, the latter representing the authentic holders of the origin.

References

Al-Rasheed, M. 2010. *A History of Saud Arabia.* Cambridge: Cambridge University Press.
Commins, D. 2006. *The Wahhabi Mission and Saudi Arabia.* New York, NY: I.B. Tauris.
Donegani, J.M. 1993. *La liberté de choisir: Pluralisme religieux et pluralisme politique dans le catholicisme français contemporain.* Paris: Presses de la FNSP.
Mouline, N. 2014. *The Clerics of Islam: Religious Authority and Political Power in Saudi Arabia.* New Haven, CT: Yale University Press.
Poulat, E. 1986. *L'Église, c'est un monde: L'ecclésiosphère.* Paris: Éditions du Cerf.

separation between the church and the state epitomized in 1905 French law and thus opposed to relegate faith to the mere private sphere. The central principle of divine unicity (*al-tawḥīd*) regards Islam not only a religious system but also a sovereign body. Salafism today similarly reacts to the absence of compliance with the Islamic principles whose scope, in their view, extends to such other spheres as spiritual, social, and political life.

CHAPTER 3

Salafism: A Brief History

Abstract This chapter has a historical focus by highlighting the main religious events and actors whose role is worth mentioning in order to understand the emergence of Salafism in Muslim societies. These different historical examples allow us to grasp some of the main debates and concepts to have in mind the contemporary political and religious issues related to the issue of Salafism.

Keywords Ahmad b. Hanbal · Muhammad b. Abd al-Wahhab · Ahmad b. Taymiyya · Fatwa · Quran · Sunna · Jihad

The desire to renew with the Ancients can nonetheless not be seen as a spontaneous process. Indeed, it was during specific crises and epochs, during which questions arose about the definition of the "true" believer and non-Muslims, the status of sin as well as the links between religion and politics, that the epistemic framework unique to Salafism was developed. It is impossible to shed light on each ordeal and event that brought partisans of a Salafist return to the head of a puritan reform movement against co-religionists guilty (in their eyes) of innovating by adding denatured aspects (*pl.: al-bida'; sing.: al-bid'a*) and threatening Islamic "original" principles. However, three figures at three different

© The Author(s), under exclusive license to Springer Nature Switzerland AG 2022
M.-A. Adraoui, *Understanding Salafism*, The Sciences Po Series in International Relations and Political Economy, https://doi.org/10.1007/978-3-031-18089-7_3

historical times can be cited as forging key moments in the affirmation of Salafist fundamentalist and restorationist ethics.

Although the Abbasid Empire (750–1258) experienced an impressive expansion, one of the consequences of which was putting Muslim communities into contact with other philosophical traditions, certain clerics (those responsible for the management of salvation assets (Weber 1993), primarily the correct interpretation of the scriptures) stand out by attempts to redefine Islam by integrating ways of reasoning that were not seen as "genuinely" Islamic back then. For example, some clerics have been inspired by Greek rationality as shown by the emergence of a branch called *muʿtazila*, one of the beliefs of which is related to the *Qurʾān* as the Word of God (*Allāh*) created on earth and not uncreated (born outside of this world). Garnering a real success, to the point that the Caliph al-Ma'mūn (786–833) decided to make it the official doctrine of his Empire in 827, it also triggered a counter-reform movement led by Aḥmad b. Ḥanbal (780–855) (Melchert 2006). The latter gave his name to one of the four schools of jurisprudence which today make up *sunnī* Islam (currently the main branch of Islam which in reality started to be formulated more specifically and rigorously in this era). A judge and legal scholar (*al-faqīh*) at the time based in Bagdad, he became known for his will to reaffirm the rights of a dogma which he considered threatened by *muʿtazilī* speculations rooted in a certain use of reason (*al-ʿaql*). He thus called to return to the faith of the Ancients and to renew with what he referred to as the Tradition (*al-naql*) made up of the *Qurʾān*, the example of the Prophet[1] and that of the *Salaf*, hence conceptualizing the importance of being part of "the people of the *sunna*" (*ahl al-sunna*), providing the first letters of nobility to *sunnī* Islam (of which Salafism can be seen as the most puritanical version). On a more political level, the cleric remained after this time a symbol of the refusal of anarchy and sedition (*al-fitna*), arguing, while spending several years imprisoned and persecuted, that an open dispute of the Caliph would lead to a political crisis without which the desired orthodoxy (right religious thought) and orthopraxy (religious and social practices led with rectitude, that is in compliance with the *Qurʾān*, the example of the Prophet and the one of the Ancients) would be threatened. Thus linking together puritan counter-reform and the preservation of the social-political order,

---

[1] This including, beyond the acts and assents of the Prophet, his words (*pl.: al-aḥadīth; sing.: al-ḥadīth*) of which Aḥmad b. Ḥanbal is a major compiler and authenticator.

he heralded quietist forms of Salafist engagement observed today in both Muslim majority and minority contexts. Fearful of the troubles and use of extreme violence[2] for the possibility of being able to practice religion, this "Great Ordeal" (*al-miḥna al-kubrā*) thus remained the occasion of vigorously defending "the true faith" which up until today marks the imaginary of Salafists (more specifically legitimist ones), who attribute the reasons that led to the survival and transmission of orthodoxy over time to his wisdom (religious wisdom gained through knowledge of the scriptures of Islam in the Salafist imaginary).

Another cleric, inheritor of the *ḥanbalī* school, stands out several centuries later by another case of puritan reform, this time turned among others against a regime accused of having not only deviated from "the right path" but having left Islam altogether. Aḥmad b. Taymiyya (1263–1328) (Rapaport and Ahmed 2015), a judge serving various Mameluke dynasties reigning over the Levant and Egypt, beyond his opposition to several forms of Sufism (even though he is a member of a brotherhood attached to this branch), *shīʿa* Islam as well as contemporary philosophers (*al-falāsifa*), is also unique for his famous legal opinion (*al-fatwā*) delivered in 1303 in the framework of this religious judgment regarding the Mongolian power fighting against Mamelukes. Seeing in the conversion of the descendants of Genghis Khān who triumphed against the Abbasid Empire and later military castes dominating at that time the Muslim East a lure, or at the very least an incomplete process, the cleric came to the (still famous) conclusion that their excommunication (*al-takfīr*) was legitimate. Their infidelity was demonstrated according to b. Taymiyya by their maintenance of the Mongolian *yasa* ("the Great Law") as the legal code under the impulsion of their leader Maḥmud Ghāzān Khān, whereas their entry into Islam should have led to only recognizing Muslim law (*al-sharīʿa*). Linking the belonging to Islam with the respect of the moral and legal injunctions he identified in the scriptures, b. Taymiyya went as far as making military combat legal against the Mongolian power which he also criticized for making a pact with Christian powers, equivalent to betrayal in his eyes. The acceptance of *jihād* (namely the effort of compliance with the principles of Islam) which he reinforced at this time is really a part of an iconoclast religious work if compared with different ordeals involving

---

[2] These explicit words are attributed to him on this subject: "Sixty years of tyranny are worth more than one night of anarchy." In another version: "Sixty years with an unjust *Sulṭān* are better than one night without a *Sulṭān*."

himself (and which led him to several years in prison), without systematically legitimizing violent combat against his enemies. The same is seen in the sentences he carried out against certain Christians. If he was one of the first to demand death penalty against ʿAsāf al Naṣrānī, a Christian who insulted the Prophet against which he demanded "to draw the sword" in 1293, or by ordering the defense of Christian "protégés" (*ahl al-dimma*) against his Mongolian enemies, by force if necessary, b. Taymiyya has been playing an important role in *sunnī* debates. His figure and exegeses having been mobilized up to the present by a number of branches, including Jihadism, in order to legitimize the use of force against any person or group supposedly "guilty" of violating the foundations of the religion.

In the eighteenth century, another cleric sought out the symbolic and moral cadaster represented by the legacy of the *salaf ṣāliḥ*. Although today the term Wahhabism (*al-wahhābiyya*) is often pinned to that of Salafism,[3] it is mainly because in the Arabian Peninsula at the time, Muḥammad b. Abd al-Wahhāb al-Tamīmī (1703–1792) (Delong Bas 2004) was seeking, in a context he deemed had become religiously heterodox, to re-establish the rights of a dogma (*al-ʿaqīda*) that he considered had been trampled on. He thus vilified and fought practices that had become usual at the time, namely the worship of graves when neither intercession (asking another to pray for oneself, which needs to be done through a direct prayer) nor veneration of any other God[4] were supposed to be part of the faith of the *Salaf*. Moreover, his puritan preaching was coupled with a political purpose by forming an alliance throughout his lifetime with Muḥammad b. Saʿūd al-Muqrin (1687–1765), tribal leader from the *Najd* area who wished to extend his power by giving him a religious unction provided by the cleric wishing to endow his fundamentalist reform with greater fighting power. Taking the form of a pact dating from 1744, in the name of which Muḥammad b. Saʿūd supported the

---

[3] Often moreover under the effect of enemies of Saudi Arabia to which they thereby wish to remove any roots in the early times of Islam in favor of a name which is supposed to "sectarize" the country by confounding Islam that is practiced with the work of a single man deprived of the prestigious genealogy coming from identification with the Ancients.

[4] The cleric condemning, for instance, the veneration of famous Muḥammad's companions at his time under the pretext that some companions and even the Prophet himself had the habit of supporting. It is thus told that Muḥammad b. Abd al-Wahhāb took down one of the most venerated trees with his bare hands, just as he asked the destruction of the grave of a famous companion and brother of the second Caliph of Islam, Zayd b. al-Khaṭṭāb, his contemporaries taking it for an object of worship.

preaching of he who became the founding religious reference of the emerging state, in exchange for his support, of the duty to govern in compliance with his opinions and defend the principle of divine unicity (*al-tawḥīd*) threatened by the "deviations" of the time, this alliance was at the origin of the first Saudi kingdom. The latter served as a model for other alliances based on this complicit transaction (Mouline 2014) between tribal chiefs and clerics, thereby illustrating a difference of roles and authorities in Muslim territory, but also a basic collusion when scholars and leaders decide to collaborate on a project combining puritan reform and political agenda. Even though it was brought down by the regional rivals, this first Saudi state came back to life on several occasions, particularly in the interwar period with the new conquest of *Ḥijāz* and the unification of the kingdom between 1926 and 1932, at the instigation of a descendant of the Saʿūd family (ʿAbd al-ʿAzīz b. Saʿūd, 1876–1953), and then again supported by the descendants of Muḥammad b. Abd al-Wahhāb (members of the al-Shaykh family which still incarnates today the religious pillar of the Saudi state), asking the latter to promote Salafism domestically as well as at a worldwide scale as this would be the case in the twentieth century.

References

Delong Bas, N. 2004. *Wahhabi Islam: From Revival and Reform to Global Jihad*. New York, NY: Oxford University Press.

Melchert, C. 2006. *Makers of the Muslim World: Ahmad Ibn Hanbal*. Oxford: Oneworld.

Mouline, N. 2014. *The Clerics of Islam: Religious Authority and Political Power in Saudi Arabia*. New Haven, CT: Yale University Press.

Rapaport, Y., and S. Ahmed. 2015. *Ibn Taymiyya and His Times*. New York: Oxford University Press.

Weber, M. 1993. *The Sociology of Religion*. Boston: Beacon Press.

CHAPTER 4

The Basics of the Salafist Ethic

Abstract This section looks at the way of reasoning and thinking about the religious in Salafist communities, highlighting in particular the role of clerics in the production of religious norms. While Salafism can be seen as a claim to read and interpret Islam in a literalist manner, this chapter illustrates the importance of religious debates and the place of a specific methodology in the way of organizing the interpretation of the principles and norms of the Muslim religion.

Keywords Clerics · Ulama · Reform

THE CLERIC, OR THE CORNERSTONE OF THE SALAFIST MEANING SYSTEM

The historical analysis of the various forms taken by the Salafist last rites, norms, and discourses reveals, despite the diversity of the issues raised over the centuries by clerics responsible for re-affirming a credo threatened by the spread of discourses and practices accused of deforming it, certain fundamental principles. Understanding Salafism can be done, at least partly, through a comparison with other reformist and fundamentalist experiences observed within other religious traditions. While it is difficult to conclude as to completely analogous forms between Salafists and *Haredis* within Judaism or integrist branches of Catholicism, it is nonetheless possible to see in the cases of the clerics discussed above certain affinities with Protestantism in Renaissance Europe. In that case where, by comparison, the debauchery as well as the abandonment of morals attributed to Popes Innocent VIII, Alexander VI, Julius II, and Leo X at the turn of the sixteenth century played a large role in the radical reaction by some theologians, first of which is Martin Luther (1483–1546). His stay in Rome (1510–1511) and particularly the sale of Indulgences (which for him represented a sin of simony, the sale of faith and salvation being an abomination) led to radically questioning the basis of Christian identity, thus generating the Reform through a rediscovery of the scriptures, Luther going as far as defying the papal institution based on the argument that only the Bible is supposed to grant authority and verity.

More or less referring to protesting forms within Islam, the use of the Salafist reference, in addition to participating in the conceptualization and formation of *sunnī* Islam, propelled clerics to the forefront of the social and political scene by establishing them as the "people of the call to order." Drawing on their claimed mastery of scriptures, these *'ulamā'* (plural of *'alīm*, or the person with knowledge, in this case of a sacred nature), some imams, legal scholars, preachers and thinkers thus paved the way that is supposed to lead back to the early times of Islam. Acting as the initiators of a call to order in an era of supposed deviance (the idea that the *Qur'ān* is the Word of God created for Aḥmad b. Ḥanbal, the lack of respect for Islamic law according to Aḥmad b. Taymiyya, or the worship of graves according to Muḥammad b. Abd al-Wahhāb), the *'ulamā'* have thus become the traditionists of Islam through which knowledge and science (*al-'ilm*) are transmitted from generation to generation,[1] these referring to the definition and the interpretation of the normative sources of Islam—namely, the *Qur'ān*, the *sunna*, the *athar*, and the opinion of clerics whether this be obtained by analogy (*al-qiyās*) with the past, consensus (*al-ijmaꜥ*) or interpretation (*al-ijtihād*).

---

[1] The principle being that for centuries clerics recommend (*al-tazkiyya*) between them and intercede (*al-wāsiṭa*) for others, illustrating this way the transmission of testimony of orthodoxy from one era to another.

Salafist clerics thus shared the desire to enforce the *episteme*[2] of the early times of Islam wherever and whenever, whether in terms of spirituality and religion or society and politics. Their main belief is that the Muslim identity is subsequently faith and practice. Unlike other historical branches (*khawārij*, *murji'a*, etc.), Muslims stand out by a faith that must be practiced with a lifestyle that is the most compliant with orthodoxy and orthopraxy as possible. Some actions can weaken the condition of the believer or even remove him from the condition when others raise him. Divine mercy is thus the only way to save the believer, but the latter must live according to a principle of permanent purification and constantly pay attention to not cross the boundaries of belief, religion, and social relations outside of which, even if they still consider himself Muslim, they will be in danger if their actions contradict the paradigm of the Ancients. Salafism is therefore a puritanism by virtue of which a tension is observed constantly between faith and practice, one theoretically nourishing the other. Debates as to the contours of a true Islamic identity explain, for that matter, a number of oppositions within Salafist communities which are thus far from forming a homogenous whole. Although the latter are united through a shared identification with the heritage of the Predecessors, the *disputatio* undeniably exists. In this respect, it seems erroneous for those wishing to understand Salafism to see a literalist form. It is more a question of scripturalism in that the content relating to the Salafist *episteme* can vary in drastic ways for instance as concerns the legitimation and conditions of the use of violence.[3] Still, Salafists remain united by an understanding of their *episteme* as a means of reasoning and as content. Any problem relating to existence must be treated according to the following axial principle: what would the Ancients have done? Only this interrogation guarantees authentically belonging to "the people of

---

[2] Which Michel Foucault (2012) means as the framework defining "the conditions of possibility of knowledge." The episteme has, according to the latter, two dimensions: one that is structural, referring to the empirical content which actors can access (in the case of Salafism the practices of the Ancients) representing an "imperceptible network of constraints"; and another that is archeological, that is, a specific way of seeing history, particular forms of producing knowledge (for Salafists by renewing with the way of reasoning of the Pious Predecessors).

[3] For the study of the differences between the quietist and Jihadist versions of Salafism, see below.

the *sunna* and the assembly" (*ahl al-sunna wal-jamāʿa*)[4] which some Salafists even consider to be "the saved group" (*al-firqat al-nājiyya*) or "the victorious faction" (*al-tā'ifa al-mansūra*), meaning that they form a community approved exclusively by God. Being founded in certain prophetic traditions (the authenticity of which as well as the meaning are, as is often the case, subject to intense debates), some followers of this last rites affirm that they are possibly the only ones to attain salvation, unlike other branches of Islam which, as sincere as they may claim to be, deviated on certain points (dogma, practice, etc.) from "the right path," thereby risking to lose divine approval.

Literalism or Scripturalism?

As a scripturalist (more than a literalist) process, the study of scriptures holds a key place. The cleric becomes thus the cornerstone of Salafist epistemic communities as he is the only to be able to translate into fact religious expectations and orders (often in the form of a *fatwā*, or an opinion given on a specific situation with a theoretically restrictive value), but also by ensuring historical and moral continuity between past centuries and the contemporary age. Although the *salaf ṣāliḥ* are the prerogative of the early times of Islam, after them certain Muslims, in what can be seen as a genealogical socialization, by choosing the path of orthodoxy as presented in this vision, can call themselves Salafists (those who follow the *salaf*). It is thus not a question of an organized political movement, even less so a party, but more so a status group first whose ambition is to exercise duties (even a hegemony) about the definition and implementation of Muslim norms, principles, and attitudes. Thus, beyond the pretention of giving specific content to the doctrine, Salafism must also be analyzed as a methodology. The sources cannot be interpreted anarchically. A certain number of ordering principles must be respected in order to establish this normative and centered Islam, beyond spiritual considerations, as to the (il)legal nature of various practices of existence. This means that Salafism is subsequently an end and a means. By providing content through clerics/*ʿulamāʾ*, this episteme refers to an offer of content as regards investiture, so as to undertake the pilgrimage to

---

[4] Expression designating Muslims on the right path, the Assembly being here a concept referring to people having followed Muhammad. Another is also used by the Salafists: "the people of the *sunna* and divine unicity" (*ahl al-sunna wal-tawḥīd*).

Mekka or political engagement after a revolutionary process in a Muslim country or withdrawal in a primarily non-Muslim society. At the same time, it is also an exegetic process of the normative sources of faith. For example, it is not surprising that many of the big historical references of Salafists, such as Aḥmad b. Ḥanbal, are also recognized as a specialist of the explanation and authentication of the *hadith*.[5] The latter did effectively count among his most famous works the collection of oral traditions of the Prophet entitled *Musnad*, for which he specifies that his approach was only possible by carefully checking if the words of Muḥammad he told were mentioned in the words of clerics preceding him and having taken the time to trace them to several companions of the Prophet, without observing any contradiction between the latter.

Finally, while the *'ulamā'* are very important in the archeology of Islamic knowledge as conceived in Salafist communities, this is because they fulfill a symbolic function of the inheritors of the Prophets. While the exceptional status of people sent by God in order to deliver His message to humanity makes it possible to evoke the existence of a metaphysical truth that is passed along by these human beings chosen to perform this mission, clerics on the other hand spread the knowledge and wisdom that are one of the manifestations of truth. Thus, they are of the greatest importance within one given society according to the Salafist imaginary. Being "the people of the call to order," they also form a specific social group that represents, at least in theory, a constant focal point for believers (all the more so when the latter are in a situation of anomy). Since the Ancients are no longer present, only *'ulamā'* can in theory claim to define "the right path" that must be taken. In practice, there are several communities of clerics, which can disagree on several points (Salafism being certainly synonymous with the intransigent conception but also with intense debates on the nature of Islam). The "rejoinder/replica/response" (*al-rudūd*) is, for instance, a central element for understanding socialization within Salafism in that it is a term that is often used to describe the *disputatio* involving certain clerics. On

---

[5] Salafist clerics historically count among those having done the most for establishing prophetic sayings as an essential root of knowledge, and more largely of Truth. By opposition to other branches which only use the *Qur'ān* for instance, or which are based on an esoteric approach to Islam, clerics recognized by Salafists largely contributed to the flourishing as well as the development of science of the *ḥadīth* (*'ilm al-ḥadīth*), who were often called the People of the hadith (*ahl al-ḥadīth*).

a given subject, one of them takes a stance and thereby triggers a debate within the space of religious deliberation that is Salafism (as long as that the conditions mentioned above are respected). Based on the rules of evidence (*al-dalīl*), drawn from the *Qur'ān* and the *sunna* according to the supposed understanding of the Pious Predecessors, this deliberation can also act as a factor of fragmentation in the Salafist field. Indeed, if the ambition of living according to the principles of the original era is capable of uniting several people, in terms of content and methods, the divergences (*al-ikhtilāfāt*) regularly accompany debates. Thus, as concerns the relationships between clerics, who are supposed to ensure the coherence of this symbolic and practical edifice, competitive or close relations can appear as part of the search for duties characterizing the Salafist reform throughout the centuries. Therefore, it is not surprising that the ties uniting the latter have led, as either a kind of dubbing or, to the contrary, cautionary statement, to praise or warnings concerning clerics whose positions can satisfy or disappoint their peers. The double tension that is fundamental to Salafist puritan reformism can be observed here: the desire to unite all Muslims on the basis of purified reading and interpretation of religious sources, and the constant quest of any behavior, discourse or stance that contradicts the claimed orthodoxy. This tension can thus lead to both a real surpassing of traditional forms of Islam (deemed non-compliant with the Ancients' practices such as the condemnation of marriage imposed on women in the name of the *sunna* which asks for the explicit agreement of the couple to be married) in the name of the unity of the dogma and original practice, and substantial divisions and even splits within Salafism as can be observed if one looks at the history and sociology of this matrix since the twentieth century.

Reference

Foucault, M. 2012. *The Order of Things: An Archeology of the Human Sciences*. New York: Vintage.

CHAPTER 5

The Globalization of Salafism

Abstract This chapter sheds light on the factors and conditions under which a real "Salafist field" emerged in the second half of the twentieth century on a global scale. Under the effect, particularly, of Saudi internal and external action, a Salafist vision of Islam became globalized. This part also puts into perspective the place and role of religious institutions within the Saudi monarchy as well as their function of moral and political legitimization of the regime.

Keywords Saudi Arabia · Wahhabism · Umma · Organization of the Islamic Conference/Cooperation · Islamic Universities · Migrations

While the different contemporary faces of Salafist reformism have become so visible, this is linked to the conjunction of several factors combining the foreign policy of some states, the reformation of the religious fabric at the national and local levels in a number of countries, the dawn and the persistence of certain conflicts involving Muslims,[1] as well as the impact of major socio-demographic changes bringing a certain number of groups

---

[1] This point will be addressed in the next chapter.

© The Author(s), under exclusive license to Springer Nature Switzerland AG 2022
M.-A. Adraoui, *Understanding Salafism*, The Sciences Po Series in International Relations and Political Economy,
https://doi.org/10.1007/978-3-031-18089-7_5

at a questioning point with their environment, and thus in search of competing narratives.

During the twentieth century, a substantial change in the geographical, cultural, and political scale occurred concerning the influence of some religious offers. Far from characterizing the unique Muslim religion, the last decades indeed enabled major upheaval in the landscape of religious belief that has become more globalized than ever. Salafism, which the events of the twentieth century contributed to reinforcing as an unavoidable religious matrix but also to fragmenting as a political ethics, specifically on the question of the relationship to established powers and the sovereignty of the *umma*, definitely incarnates this phenomenon.[2] These evolutions benefited from several factors that made it possible to understand the structuring of a global Salafist field, namely a sociological sphere at once bringing together and opposing actors with the pretention of embodying orthodoxy in the wake of identification with the Ancients.

The Statization of Salafism with the Birth and the Rise of Modern Saudi Arabia

First of all, the globalization of Salafism fully benefitted from the historical and religious specialization claimed by the current Saudi Arabia kingdom, namely the defense of a "genuine" form of Islam, which its important economic (the primary producer and exporter of fossil fuels) and symbolic resources (the country being the geographical birthplace of Islam) enable it to consider as an important dimension of its international action. If Salafism, for which we have seen the usefulness of the topographical metaphor for grasping its content, seems (at least for some) to have made a home for itself in the Gulf, and particularly in Saudi Arabia, this is because of the preaching dimension that characterizes both the internal and external policies of this monarchy since at least the second half of the twentieth century. While it is difficult to compare with the action of a Westphalian state whose national interest is mainly dependent on the preservation of its security and the maximization of its power, Saudi Arabia since its origins has a fundamental relationship with the narrative

---

[2] Term which comes from the root *u-m* which means "motherhood." Often translated by "community/nation of believers", this notion refers rather to the idea of a motherhood of Muslims, that certain militant groups want to unite under a single political and religious sovereignty (see below).

of the defense of Islam and Muslims, for which it is not only a question of coming to their aid when circumstances require but which are also the subjects of their fundamentalist reformism as demonstrated by a number of events.

If the quest for the duties over "genuine" Islamic principles that have historically been the responsibility of some clerics, doubles for understanding the landscape of contemporary Salafism of the search for Saudi political leadership within what is generally described as the Muslim world, religious considerations are not absent. By ensuring the diffusion of a doctrine through some specific channels that has legitimized for several centuries the undertaking of state construction by the Saud, the kingdom is assured of being a vector of influence and identity that it has never hesitated to mobilize in its international action. This influence has moreover been reinforced by the ideological animosity at the head of this country for several decades for nationalist, communist, liberal, revolutionary, and more recently Islamist and Jihadist theses.[3]

Several spaces of influence and preaching have thus emerged following the 1960s in the aim of reinforcing what appears to be a "State-sponsored Salafism," embodying since then one of the main faces of the search for orthodoxy during our time. This is the case of the transnational institutional networking which the kingdom is at the root of with the creation in 1969 of an inter-governmental body, the *Organization of the Islamic Conference* (which became the *Organization of the Islamic Cooperation* in 2011), with headquarters in Jeddah and created with the explicit aim of defending the holy sites of Islam, triggering the diplomatic and economic cooperation between Muslim countries and coming to the aid of co-religionists, starting with the Palestinian people, the OIC (today composed of 57 states) being created notably after an Australian Christian fundamentalist set the *al-ʿAqsā'* Mosque on fire in Jerusalem on August 21, 1969. Although the political context that presides for Saudi Arabia, seeking a transnational Muslim unity, has a lot to do with the desire to counter Arabism and third-world nationalism heralded by the Egyptian President Jamal ʿAbd al-Nāsir, one of the aims of the OIC is to defend the Islamic vision of ethical, legal, and international political challenges (human rights, family organization, religious freedoms, etc.). Several years earlier in 1962, another non-governmental organization, the

---

[3] See below.

World Islamic League, emerged with the aim of spreading pan-Islamic theses (already in opposition with Nasserian pan-Arabism) and promoting the Muslim faith in all its dimensions (construction of religious sites, funding of humanitarian projects, working to unite the Muslim people, building schools and religious institutions, etc.). Established at *Mekka*, under the authority of a secretary general who is often Saudi, the League is nonetheless not restricted to majority Muslim countries, as illustrated by their participation in building religious sites in Western countries such as the Grand Mosque in Mantes-la-Jolie near Paris, constructed in the 1980s, which still houses today the French offices of the League, or the Grand Mosque in Lyon inaugurated in 1994 (and funded not only by them but also by a personal donation from King Fahd (1921–2005) at the head of the monarchy at the time).

The university channel also represents, beyond the strategy of institutional networking at the global level, an important means of exporting the Salafist imaginary to the world. Since the 1960s, the Islamic universities of *Mekka*, *Madīna*, and Riyadh have trained several generations of students in the conception of orthodoxy valued in Saudi Arabia. If these institutions cannot be restricted to their proselytizing function, they have nonetheless contributed to training and socializing thousands of students funded by the Saudi State, whose returns to their countries of origin have consolidated the dynamic of globalization of Salafism during the twentieth century (Farquhar 2016). The same can be observed concerning migratory waves toward the Golf that have connected several generations of workers that went to these developing countries starting in the 1970s (in the wake of the explosion of oil prices) and lived in proximity of Saudi State-sponsored Salafism.

These human and migratory streams thus contributed to the globalization of a religious imaginary which had been circulating prior to that the time primarily among political and religious elites in the Muslim world. If, indeed, the analysis of Salafism tends to focus (not without reason) on the religious debate as well as the use of the latter in political and ideological struggles for power and hegemony as concerns Islamic norms (the relation between princes and clerics often providing the angle from which Salafism is envisioned), studying the contours of this reformist and fundamentalist ambition using the prism of social history makes it possible to widen the understanding of the various phenomena at stake. The presence of Salafist communities in a Muslim-minority country, for instance, is often due to the preaching of young imams many of which were trained in the Gulf, but for others also aware of this branch in other Muslim countries (Mauritania, Syria, Jordan, etc.) where Salafism had spread long before reaching the West, South-East Asia, or Western Africa. Often through nomadic imams preaching intermittently in different mosques, without considering the rise of the internet since the 1990s as a space of a territorial resonance and socialization, where web sites and social networks fully play their role of eliminating the geographical distance and time difference to the benefit of instantaneousness, numerous countries have discovered Salafism (and vice versa) mainly through the role of micro-communities acting through preaching in a decentralized way, namely without a conscious global strategy. A phenomenon which is in a way first of all cultural, the appropriation by certain people worldwide of the codes of the Salafist last rites echoes a veritable globalization of the margins (even though this is unquestionably fed by the action of certain States, Saudi Arabia primarily). At the same time, additional factors have played a significant role. The Algerian conflict during the 1990s also contributed to reinforcing the visibility of this puritanism in French society for instance in that a number of imams crossed the Mediterranean Sea in order to settle in the former colonizing power. Embodying in this way a case of globalization of religion since the twentieth century, Salafism, by being situated at the crossroads of a logic of exportation centered on a state, and a dynamic of globalization in terms of identity more than politics, is as much the product of an inter-social relationship as of an inter-state one. Resulting from a reticular logic before becoming state-centered, the sociology of globalized Salafism thus escapes from simplifying views reducing its current weight only to a proselytizing aim decided by a foreign government.

THE SAUDIZATION OF SALAFISM IN THE TWENTIETH CENTURY: WHEN SAUDI ARABIA SPEAKS FOR ISLAM AND THE *UMMA*

The dawn of new countries in the first half of the twentieth century did not only mean the emergence of new states but also the arrival of new narratives on the world stage. Saudi Arabia built itself as a state with a "manifest Islamic destiny," echoing the need to bring greatness back to the Muslim religion after centuries of decline which is explained within Salafism by a distancing from "orthodox" Islam. Establishing a missionary state for co-religionists who need support and "the right word and path," Saudi Arabia uses discourse and action defined by the belief that the country (starting with its political and religious elites) and Islam are enmeshed in their values and interests.

This quest for duties over the *umma* led to an essential consequence. Saudi Arabia established its legitimacy for nearly a century in the service of "authentic" Islam, thus running the risk of seeing religious symbolism turned against it in the case of a "breach" of its historical specialization echoed in its preaching and missionary role. The latter, which has over the past several decades took the form of funding for the foundation of religious sites across the world, the organization of an educational and university system based on the promotion of Salafist norms, an institutional network with a transnational dimension in view of bringing together all Muslim states, and even support for *sunnī* ideological movements and armed groups engaged in domestic or international struggles in defense of Muslims, has tried to mold the global Islamic field in its image, thus risking to see alliances turn against it if the religious legitimacy of the kingdom gets disputed.

A Two-Level State Salafism: Clerics and Kings

This nationalization of Salafism connected with the Saudi preaching state is first based on a doctrinal clarification, theorized, and guaranteed by the clerics. As an intransigent conception of Islam, whose aim is the revival of a dogma, a religion, and social relations which would have been supposedly observed in the early times of Islam, Salafism as affirmed by the Saudi state is organized around the need to swear allegiance (*al-walā'*) to regimes claiming Islam, no matter how imperfect, or run the risk of triggering sedition (*al-fitna*) without which no orthodoxy can exist. The discipline of the state alone can, in this perspective, guarantee the stability and security that are seen as the *sine qua non* condition of an acceptable religious observance. Disavowal (*al-barā'*) of a religiously imperfect regime can only be done if the clerics decide, which means that they are in theory the true holders of authority in that they grant kings, presidents, or governments Islamic legitimacy, or take it away. In the tradition of this dual authority, theoretically subject to the primacy of clerics (*al-'ulamā'*), if a political power is considered seriously refuting their religious duties (wrong international alliances, tolerance of laws deemed incompatible with Islam, moral debauchery, etc.), and if "the good advice" (*al-naṣīḥa*) of clerics does not bear fruit, permission can be granted to revolt against this "corrupt" regime. By means of a vehement and dissenting understanding of *jihād* (an effort to become compliant with the principles of Islam), certain believers can claim to return to "original" Islam through an undertaking that is not only politicized, but also revolutionary in that the violent insurrection becomes legitimate against the religiously inept authority[4] that sometimes go as far as excommunicating (*al-takfir*).

In the Saudi case, the definition of true politics (namely that which is in line with divine law (*al-sharī'a*) and the interest of Muslims, whether Saudi or not) is done by official institutions which organize what is possible to see as a form of State Salafism by virtue of which a body of clerics established and then co-opted, guide the Saudi government policy and state system (most often formed by members of the Sa'ūd monarchy). On the one hand, the *Committee of the Great Scholars* (founded in 1971), today directed by the Grand *muftī* Abd al-'Azīz Āl-Shaykh (born in 1940, a descendant of Muḥammad b. Abd al-Wahhāb), the main religious body that is dedicated to the Islamic approval of political decisions as well as providing religious counsel, above all to the king, who embodies the secularized arm of power. On the other hand, the *Permanent Delegation for Islamic Research and the Issuance of* Fatāwā, also directed by the Grand *muftī* and dedicated to giving religious consultations, not only for society concerning varied questions such as religious practice, private legal affairs (marriage, divorce, inheritance, etc.), or the kingdom's foreign policy, but also for research and education (via the management of institutions attached to the Delegation). These various bodies are characterized by their solidarity with the monarchy, particularly when the latter is attacked by other states or other Islamic movements which consider that the politics led by Saudi Arabia contradict these fundamental values. Two famous examples illustrate the solidarity linking the royal family and the body of official *'ulamā'* at the summit of the monarchy. First, the campaign against the Muslim Brotherhood in the wake of the 1991 Gulf War, which resulted in the kingdom asking U.S. protection against Iraq, the Islamist branch targeting the Saudi policy of cooperating with the West to the detriment of their "natural" duty of distrust toward countries that are "enemies of Islam." A *fatwā* issued by the Grand *muftī* at the time thus clearly took a stance against the Muslim Brotherhood, which he criticized

---

[4] *Jihād* is not only here a call to reason and morality but also a fight led with the sword (*jihād bi-l-sayf*) to re-establish the rights of the dogma.

for their inclination for sedition and the weakening of established regimes, particularly the Saudi regime, his opinion being that social order must absolutely be preserved and thus not subject to religious criticism, the state having done what it had to do. Then, still following the crisis triggered by the invasion of Kuwait by Saddam Hussein's *baʿthī*[5] regime, the hostility, still alive and well today, opposing the Saudi regime supported by official religious institutions with Jihadist influences (yet themselves still wishing to revive the Ancient heritage[6]) took the form of an anathema directed on the royal family criticized for its "hypocrisy," symbolized by its acts of "betrayal" such as the alliance with the United States and the presence of its troops on land housing the two holiest Islamic Sanctuaries (*bilād al-ḥaramayn*), namely *Mekka* and *Madīna*. A number of *fatāwā*, issued in particular by the Grand *muftī* at the time, Abd al-ʿAzīz b. Bāz (1910–1999), one of whose unique traits is the (exceptional) fact that he was not a member of the al-Shaykh family, clearly aiming to disqualify these movements claiming a violent vision of *jihād*, thus emerged to counter the discourse of the *al-Qāʿida* organization. Moreover, this campaign continues today in that the Islamic State Organization is still condemned in the same way, with Jihadist branches being accused of pointless bloodshed and spreading anarchy worldwide.

Reference

Farquhar, M. 2016. *Circuits of Faith: Migration, Education and the Wahhabi Mission*. Stanford, CA: Stanford University Press.

---

[5] "Baathist."

[6] See below.

CHAPTER 6

The Fragmentation and Crisis of Salafism: The Saudi Turn and the Rise of New Ideological Contenders

Abstract This chapter looks at the fragmentation of Salafism from the late 1970s and particularly through the Gulf crisis of the early 1990s. By showing the changes in Saudi Arabia's political and religious role, this section explains why this monarchy has been at the heart of major reconfigurations of the global Salafist landscape for several decades.

Keywords Salafist-Jihadism · Usama b. Laden · Al-Qaeda · Islamist Consensus · Gulf War · Arab Spring · Legitimist Salafism

From Consensus to Crisis of Legitimacy: The Fragmentation and Explosion of the Global Salafist Field Around the Question of the Sa'ud. The Challenge of Islamism, Jihadism, and Democratization

From an Offensive Salafism to a Defensive Form of Salafism

A certain number of historical events pushed Saudi Arabia to revise the ideological content which nonetheless defined its religious identity for decades, during which the kingdom had a near monopoly within the Salafist global landscape. Even though it is a missionary state, Saudi Arabia had to switch to a form of Salafism that can be characterized as "defensive," due to evolutions and changes that have marked the Islamic design of the Saudi kingdom after 1945. If, from a domestic point of view, the doctrine has been expressed since the birth of the third Saudi kingdom by a strong conservatism in terms of morals and legislation, the Saudi international policy has demonstrated real dynamism, especially if we keep in mind the historic alliance of 1945. The main oil-producing country and the American superpower, soon to be victorious over Nazi Germany, represented by King ʿAbd al-ʿAzīz b. Saʿūd and President Franklin Delano Roosevelt (1882–1945), signed on February 14, 1945, on the *Quincy* war ship an alliance that is today the basis of the Saudi monarchy's foreign policy. Taking advantage of the religious legitimacy granted by the body of the *'ulamā'*, whose principles emphasize the abomination of disputing a political order claiming Islam, as well as the American protection granted against a supply of oil in the best possible conditions, the country was able to promote an effective policy. Religious proselytism, creating a true Saudi *soft power*, supportive of the incumbent power and conservative at the domestic level, dynamic and serving the image of the country at the international level, and supported by economic force bolstered by the rise in the price of oil during the 1970s, is at the heart of the political-religious contract that ensured the country a privileged position on the world stage. This double movement of economic and religious development enables the puritan religiosity identified with the form of Islam practiced in Saudi society to gain true prestige across the Muslim world. The two-pronged Saudi regime moreover never hesitated to wield the most "authentic" religious rhetoric in order to disqualify its political and ideological adversaries within and outside of the state, the preaching role serving each time to bolster the credibility of Saudi positions.

Domestically, this is for instance the case during the taking of *Mekka*, which was finally aborted but attempted by a commando led by a religious radical opponent named *Juhayman Al- ʿUtaybī* (Hegghammer and Lacroix 2011). On November 20, 1979, they tried to overthrow the monarchy accused of already being "falsely" interested by authentic Islam, as shown by the problematic mores of certain princes in private, the American alliance on the international level, and the socio-cultural modernization that the country was undergoing following the oil shocks.

Internationally, the Nasserian competition insisting on reference to Arabism grew in the 1960s when the Saudi kingdom insisted on religious belonging as the cement joining the people of the Muslim world. After 1979, another competitor emerges, Khomeinist Iran, which will try to represent this religion by disqualifying Saudi Arabia, the "slave" of the "American Satan" and thus "traitor of Islam." It is moreover the revolutionary *Shīʿa* and Iranian pressure which explains in large part Saudi Arabia's investment in the Afghan conflict after 1979, with the *muftī* of the kingdom, Abd al-ʿAzīz Ibn Bāz, decreeing the country "land of armed *jihād*" for all Muslims worldwide. The Saudi state, beyond the religious dimension thus added to the conflict, took back a part of the Iranian rise obtained in the name of a revolution, one of the slogans of which was "Death to America!". On another level, to signify the religious predominance of the Saudi monarch, in 1986, the latter added the "Guardian of the Holy Sanctuaries" of Islam *(khādim al-ḥaramayn al-sharīfayn)* to his sovereign title, with Iran sending each year "pilgrim-activists" responsible for undermining the symbolic authority of the monarchy in the most sacred sites of Islam (Kepel 2003a).

The "blessed period," when the strategic and religious bet gave the impression of succeeding, coincided with a religious conception that can be seen as both dynamic and extensive. While the Islamic principles defended were Salafist, the leaders attached to the religious authority were not included in the logic of blame that characterized the official clerics since the Gulf War of 1991 in particular. The Saudi strategy is more similar in this era to a quest to expand the country's audience. As such, these elements of similarity and of political-religious synergy prevail, as illustrated by King Fayṣal's (1906–1975) outstretched hand to the Muslim Brotherhood (Lia 1999), persecuted by the Nasserian power after 1954, or the funding of movements drawing on *sunnī* rhetoric in order to use violence to defend certain "Muslim causes."[1] The Saudi State doctrine is satisfied by the emulation that is observed as part of a true "consensus" according to which Saudi clerics accepted, despite strictly

---

[1] We know for instance that even before the beginning of the war in Afghanistan, the Saudi State helped the Pakistani military regime in its historical rivalry with India, thereby enabling the very birth of the Taliban movement. These "students of religion", adopting an ultra-puritanical view whose doctrine is drawn from the *wahhābī* rigorism and the preaching of Deobandi groups, themselves fundamentalist as they sought the revival of the Muslim faith in a "purified" way, played the role we know about in the 1990s in their support of *al-Qāʿida*.

religious disputes, the political connections between the Saudi power and other pan-Islamic movements, provided that the Saud leadership is not disputed. Placing, in a way, the Saudi national political interest before a strict observance of dogmatic prescriptions, these years are ones of the greatest trans-Islamic legitimacy of the Saudi kingdom within the religious landscape[2] that it largely contributed to establishing.

The Emergence of Salafism-Jihadism and the Crisis of Saudi Religious and Political Legitimacy

This "syncretic moment" (Adraoui 2020) within *sunnī* Islam, yet oriented for several decades toward the consolidation of a global Islamic identity under Saudi leadership results, ended in a return to an ultra-legitimist discourse (Piscatori 1991) due to political changes putting Saudi Arabia at risk. This is why the religious authority increasingly integrated, more than in the past, the constraints weighing on Saudi power due to the splitting of the Salafist sphere under the effect of Usāma b. Lāden's efforts to undermine the monarchy's legitimacy in particular. In this respect, an event marks a decisive turn in the official Saudi position materialized by a severe split within the Salafist field between "revolutionaries" and "legitimists." This basic tension starting with the Gulf crisis in 1990 represents another illustration of the organic link between political power and religious authority at the head of the Saudi State. The even larger solidarity between the two pillars of the system produced a radical switch in discourse comparing notably those who committed the abomination of turning against the Saudi rulers seen as the legitimate governors of the country to "fake Salafists." The "Islamic consensus[3]" (Piscatori 1991)

---

[2] King Fayṣal chose for instance after the 1960s to facilitate access to religious teaching for Egyptian Muslim Brotherhood activists which, later, in doctrinal terms, resulted in the emergence (or re-emergence) of an ultra-rigorist, potentially revolutionary political-religious view, including toward the Saudi regime, which had been considered up until then as the main support of Islamic movements worldwide. *Al-Qāʿida* and Usāma b. Lāden are certainly the most well-known avatars of this hybridization of "Salafist-Wahhabist" canons by the militant conception of the Muslim Brotherhood, many of which were radicalized in the context of violent interaction with the Nasserian power.

[3] This expression designates the political and religious configuration which had ensured a central place in Saudi Arabia for several decades up until the crisis opened by the invasion of Kuwait by Saddam Hussein's armies on August 2, 1990. The Islamist consensus refers to the Saudi hegemony which is accepted as beneficial by a majority of Muslim activist groups and movements within the global Islamic sphere.

that was the source of the centrality granted to Saudi Arabia found itself undermined by the action of de-legitimation undertaken by the "revolutionary" Salafists (Salafists-Jihadists), who were moreover also presenting themselves as the defenders of "authentic" Islam. Seen by revolutionary Salafists as blind to the need to fight, if need be through armed conflict, for the benefit of the Muslim people throughout the world, "the clerics of the palace" *('ulamā al-balāṭ)* have since been vilified for abandoning what represents for Jihadists the heart of the preaching, namely the Islamization of power and legislation.[4] The same clerics, on the other hand, came to the aid of Saudi power by virtue of their conservative understanding of Islam. The presence of foreign troops, particularly Americans, in the country housing the sacred sites of Islam constitutes the reason for which "the winners of Afghanistan" (i.e., the first generation of Salafist-Jihadists) went after the monarchy, updating in their perspective "the duplicity and hypocrisy" of the latter (Gerges 2011). The defense of Islam needing from then on to return to this vanguard having better understood the widespread hate against Islam than the establishment clerics; it is now a matter of disqualifying the Saudi two-thronged power.

It is thus in this logic of mutual discredit, reaching a level of anathema particularly on the Jihadist side, which spoke of "apostate regimes" (Hegghammer 2010), that the fragmentation must be understood which had become central in the Saudi political and religious landscape as well as in several Muslim countries. If one of the main consequences of this crisis of legitimacy is the stronger rigor with which the legitimist and anti-revolutionary canons were spread to the whole Islamic field (Kepel 2003), these two facets of contemporary Salafism were split.

While legitimist Salafists opt for an undisputable faithfulness to Saudi power since the beginning of important uprisings and deep political transitions in the Arab world in 2011, which went as far as approving the reinforcement of the U.S. alliance, and even with Israel, on the basis of a shared fear of the Iranian expansion and the growing influence of Jihadist movements within some Arab countries, the latter targeted more

---

[4] It is for this reason the revolutionaries pejoratively call the legitimist religious scholars, "clerics of the menses" (*'ulamā al-ḥayḍ*), to imply that the object of their teaching neglects the essential, namely Islamic morality regarding the exercise of political power, focusing instead on topics they consider marginal, as illustrated here by the reference to women's intimacy.

than ever the Saudi kingdom accused of betraying the role defender of co-religionists on which it had been constructed.

SINCE THE ARAB REVOLUTIONS: SAUDI ARABIA BETWEEN POSITIVE AND NEGATIVE CENTRALITY

The above-mentioned phenomena are verified by the revolts in the Arab world which started in the winter of 2010 and which led notably to the fall of Presidents Ben ʿAlī in Tunisia and Mubārak in Egypt before generating several conflicts (Syria, Libya, etc.) and authoritarian revivals and restorations. Once again vehicles of conservatism and legitimacy in the name of religion in a situation of dispute, the official Saudi clerics united with the other side of the Saudi two-thronged power, removing any Islamic aspect from "the Arab Spring." This is evident in the order given during the manifestations impacting Saudi Arabia in March 2011, which resulted not only in a return to the religious order, indicating disapproval of these events, but especially a leaping to the defense of the regime as an organic support of Islam[5]:

> "The Council of Grand Scholars beseeches Allāh to grant all Muslims aid, stability, and the unification of governors and the governed around the Truth. The Council praises Allah for having granted the Kingdom of Saudi Arabia the favor of reuniting his word and uniting his ranks around the Book of Allāh and the Tradition of the Prophet in the shadow of a wise governance, legitimized by a legal allegiance, that Allāh grants him strength and longevity and that Allāh completes for us this good deed and makes it last.
> (…)
> Allāh grants the people of this country to come together, with their governors, around the guidance of the Book and Tradition, without making them diverge or to spread their word according to other branches coming from elsewhere, or parties with antagonist principles.
> (…)
> The Kingdom has succeeded in conserving this Islamic identity. Thus, despite the progress and development that the Kingdom has experienced, and the recourse to legal terrestrial ways, it does not permit, nor will it

---

[5] http://www.as-salafs.com/2011/03/21/le-comite-des-grands-savants-exhorte-au-maintien-de-lunion-et-souligne-la-prohibition-des-manifestations/ [Accessed 4 November 2021].

ever permit—by the Force of Allāh and His Power—branches with ideas coming from the West or East to undermine this identity or disperse the Assembly."

This excerpt cannot be understood without putting it in perspective with Salafist-Jihadist texts for whom this country is today an enemy of Islam. One text is interesting from this point of view for illustrating the "ambiguous" or "dual" dimension that was the Salafist norm in the twentieth century and which explains why this religious field exploded after the 1990s. It is an article from a *takfīrī* (follower of excommunication) website which cites "the sins" committed by leaders of this country:

"The impiousness of Saudi Arabia takes on several forms, such as the seat at the UN General Assembly, the organization of municipal elections, the authorization of interests in international transactions: the amendment of martial law concerning military flight which is subject to months in prison, member state of UNESCO (acceptance of the charter, etc.), the bearing of the cross of King Fahd; the alliance with American infidels, their fight against *muwaḥidīn* [reference to Jihadists].

The alliance with the infidels: the abandonment of *jihād* and the alliance with infidels against the Taliban and the Iraqis, the presence of U.S. bases in Arabia, their fighter planes bomb Muslims, as well as giving gifts and food to soldiers, without mentioning the oil that they sell to these infidels."[6]

This excerpt supports the essential idea that Saudi Arabia is at the heart of tensions which have marked the Salafist field after the wars in Afghanistan and Iraq at the turn of the 1990s. Split in two, due in particular to the judgment to adopt toward the Saudi monarchy, each side is Saudi-centered in a sense, whether it positively or negatively by congratulating or blaming this state for defending or betraying the "true" version of Salafism.

The Salafist narrative continues today to provide the ideological shield thanks to which the Saudi state tries to neutralize the effects of the policy of defending Islam, which it nonetheless triggered since the mid-twentieth century. The collision of these two branches (legitimist-Salafist and Jihadist-Salafist) since the Gulf crisis constitutes, without being the

---

[6] http://tawhid-wa-al-jihad.over-blog.com/article-25372538.html [Accessed 14 December 2021].

only one, one of the major keys for understanding the dynamics underway in the Muslim world. Thus, it is now clear that a crucial difference distinguishes the political and religious fields characterizing contemporary Muslim societies impacted by Salafist attitudes compared to what prevailed in the 1960s, namely that by stopping from sponsoring Islamic movements across the world, Saudi Arabia that was at once one of the chief actors legitimizing militant and radical Islam has now become one of their most serious opponents since the early 1990s (Al-Rasheed 2007; Lacroix 2011). The dual character of Saudi Arabia, pushing it to be a Westphalian state creating alliances and counter-alliances according to its interests, as well as a preaching actor having led for decades a global religious re-affirmation seeking to reintroduce the symbolic aspect of Islam in world political struggles, thus seems to have given an additional target for Jihadist movements by choosing to remain faithful to what is seen as the American *imperium*. By brandishing its State-sponsored Salafism to de-legitimize Jihadist activism, the Saudi monarchy thus largely contributed to the fragmentation of Islamic radicalism in the contemporary era (Aarts and Roelants 2015), thereby illustrating that some of these prior instigators could, in the very name of fundamentalism, join the opposition to contemporary Jihadism.

THE RISE OF A "SOFT SALAFISM": RELIGIOUS REFORMATION IN SAUDI ARABIA?

The coming to power of King Salmān b. Saʿūd (born in 1935), reinforced since 2017 by the appointment of his son and now crown prince, Muḥammad b. Salmān (born in 1985), seems to formalize a turning point in religious discourse aimed at the rest of the world. This had been present for several years, but it now seems to be a question of real positions involving all of Saudi power. Regarding more particularly the image of Islam that it wishes to give while Jihadism, Arab revolutions, Islamist successes and Western pressures weigh on the sustainability of the kingdom, Saudi Arabia, in particular through the World Islamic League and the main religious figures of the country, seems to lay the foundations for a less rigorous Salafism. In order to reform society but also to put an end to the accusations of duplicity weighing on the Saudi power, new axes of religious discourse are put forward as can be seen in the speeches of Muḥammad ʿAbd al-Karīm Al-ʿIsā, new secretary general of the World Islamic League. He now calls on Muslims established in

Western societies to consider themselves full citizens of their countries, to fight against religious radicalism and to promote inter-religious dialogue. If this does not mean that the Salafism centered for decades on the Saudi political and religious authorities has definitely lost its rigorous dimension, these recent developments nonetheless show a greater overlap than ever with the current domestic authoritarian turn as well as possibilities for reform according to the national and international configurations with which Saudi Arabia must deal.

References

Aarts, P., and C. Roelants. 2015. *Saudi Arabia. A Kingdom in Peril*. New York, New York: Oxford University Press.

Adraoui, M.A. 2020. *Salafism Goes Global: From the Gulf to the French Banlieues*. New York: Oxford University Press.

Al-Rasheed, M. 2007. *Contesting the Saudi State. Islamic Voices from a New Generation*. Cambridge: Cambridge University Press.

Gerges, F.A. 2011. *The Rise and Fall of Al-Qaeda*. Oxford: Oxford University Press.

Hegghammer, T., and Lacroix, S. 2011. *The Meccan Rebellion: The Story of Juhayman al-'Utaybi Revisited*. Amal Press.

Hegghammer, T. 2010. *Jihad in Saudi Arabia. Violence and Pan-Islamism since 1979*. Cambridge: Cambridge University Press.

Kepel, G. 2003. *Jihad: The Trail of Political Islam*. Cambridge, MA: Harvard University Press.

Lacroix, S. 2011. *Awakening Islam. The Politics of Religious Dissent in Contemporary Saudi Arabia*. Cambridge, MA: Harvard University Press.

Lia, B., 1999. *The Society of the Muslim Brothers in Egypt: The Rise of an Islamic Mass Movement*. Ithaca Press.

Piscatori, J. 1991. *Islamic Fundamentalism and the Gulf Crisis*. American Academy of Arts and Sciences, Fundamentalism Project.

CHAPTER 7

Salafism and Modernity: Beyond Politics

Abstract This chapter focuses on lesser-known sociological aspects of Salafism today. Beyond strictly religious, political, and even security considerations, Salafist communities are far from being reducible to questions about their alleged dangerousness. In terms of economic ethics, the role of salutary migration to Muslim countries for Salafists living in a minority Muslim society or the relationship with traditional religious authorities, the sociology of contemporary Salafism reflects many features that make it possible to see, beyond the apparent opposition between fundamentalism and modernity, this current of Islam as both the product and a vector of modernity in a large number of situations.

Keywords Hijra/Religious migration · Economic success · Salvation · Crisis of traditional authority · Culture and religion

Crisis of Traditional Authority and Divorce Between Culture and Religion

One of the most notable evolutions of the landscape of belief in Muslim territory and beyond is certainly that of the religious authority considered as traditional. Indeed, even though Saudi Arabia has for several decades developed institutions whose key mission is to manage the political and social affairs of the kingdom with a right of oversight and good advice *(al-naṣīḥa)* to the monarchy when it seems to the clerics that the decisions made can be more strongly compliant with religious orders at the domestic or international levels, Salafism is elsewhere more often an exterior actor to the official religious apparatus.

Understanding the religious, sociological, and political content inherent to this fundamentalist reformism leads us to observe several levels of identification. In the Saudi context, Salafism must be seen in its institutionalized form and organically linked to the monarchical power (Mouline 2014; Ismail 2021). The best proof of this is the shared authority of clerics and kings/princes (essentially coming from the Saʿūd family) in line with the founding pact of 1744, which leads to the institutionalization and officialization of a religious body bringing together the main clerics of the Saudi kingdom, with the Grand *muftī*[1] at the head (a position created in 1953) whose opinions and sentences have played an essential role in the rise of a certain number of Islamic movements for several decades.[2] As we have previously seen, the body of the clerics is thus institutionalized at the head of the Saudi state in two complementary entities. On the one hand, *hayāt kibār al- ʿulamāʾ*, i.e., the Committee of Great Scholars (founded in 1971) directed by the Grand *muftī* Abd al-ʿAzīz Āl-Shaykh (a descendant of Muḥammad b. Abd al-Wahhāb), the main religious body, dedicated to the Islamic approval of political decisions as well as the religious advice provided to leaders, the king in the first place, embodying the secularized dimension of power. On the other hand, *al-lajnat dāʾima li-l-buḥūth wa al-iftā*, i.e., the Permanent Delegation for Islamic Research and the Issuance of *Fatāwā*, also directed by the Grand *muftī* and dedicated to the provision of religious consultations on potentially any domain requiring a political decision from the King.

On the other hand, the majority of Muslim countries (without evoking societies that are majority non-Muslim) are distinguished by a substantially different configuration to the extent that religious intuitions are not, since notably the period of independence where Islam, according to the country, played a variable role in political movements, explicitly based on the Salafist renewal. This is why Salafism plays a different role

---

[1] Whose title comes from the same linguistic root as the term for the term *fatwā*.
[2] See below.

in other geographical and cultural contexts than it does in Saudi Arabia. Salafists in Western societies for example interpret their entry into this puritan career as an opposition to the values and norms of a supposedly modern society; Salafism in historically Muslim territory may in this case be understood as the framework of resistance to illegitimate forms of religious organization, whether in terms of content or a claimed identity. Put differently, the weight of Salafist codes in socio-cultural contexts as diverse as Morocco, Nigeria, Egypt, Kosovo, and Indonesia is part of a broader phenomenon of the crisis of religious authority by virtue of which a form of national identity steeped in Islam, and the local context in which Islam prospered was built for several centuries. Often cited as a case in point on this topic, the teaching and discourse of a key traditional institution, i.e., the University of *al-Azhar* in Egypt, today increasingly in competition with new more globalized branches of Islam on its soil that claim to represent the orthodoxy notwithstanding the socio-cultural configuration in which they are now present, have growing difficulties to convince social groups fully in the process of sociological modernization and globalization. Among the numerous consequences of this evolution is the distrust of conceptions considered as traditional or religious that Salafist narratives profit from. This disconnection between religion and culture (Roy 2014) is at the heart of dynamics of disaffiliation that particularlyz affect generations that have experienced the switch in their societies to (almost) mass literacy (at least in the urban context) as well as individualism, phenomena which make the adhesion to traditional and inherited forms of religiosity more difficult. To these groups that are sociologically modernized, Salafism offers a narrative that is definitely fundamentalist but also (and maybe especially) adapted to the desire to rationalize religiosity whether in terms of dogma and religion or social and moral discourse. Salafism finds a fertile ground in these situations where approach focusing on mental topography provides a structured answer to situations of anomy linked to the generational changes as well as the incompatibility between Islam handed down by past generations and modern sociological conditions. Mass education, for instance, reinforces the potential of criticism by contemporary cohorts by providing the possibility of defying traditional clerics by direct reading and exegesis of scriptures, something that was impossible in the past when literacy was not so widespread.

Islam of Globalization? When Fundamentalism is Modern

This dissonance between local culture and the form of globalized Islam that is Salafism explains also why the latter, to the surprise of observers who were astonished by the success of an intransigent religious identity not only in regions as diverse as the Arab world, Southeast Asia, Western Africa, Central Asia or Western Europe, but also among different non-confessional origins (the share of converts in Western contexts being very important and which continues to be striking[3]), takes advantage of various social and cultural dynamics of globalization. Based on the idea that Islam is a simple dogma to assimilate thanks to the meditation of authorized clerics which put believers in the path of those from prestigious generations (contemporary with Muḥammad), this reformism also stands out by its claim to be "purely" religious in not only the doctrinal sense but also on a social and cultural level. Calling believers notably through the dialectic of the legal *(al-ḥalāl)* and the illegal *(al-ḥarām)* by which the environment is tamed, each society is from then on able to welcome a fundamentalist narrative which appears identical everywhere that it is implemented. Not being dependent on a local or national culture, the "pure" religiosity that is Salafism can more easily touch the hearts and souls of people to whom it is no longer asked to choose between, for instance, Arabization, and westernization, but to first assimilate before anything else a moral which is constant in time and space. Furthermore, Salafist communities demonstrate in practice a compatibility with several modern values at the sociological level. This is true for some codes of liberal globalization (appetite for mass consumer society if it respects the prohibitions of Islam and the emphasis on the spirit of capitalism if it involves morally acceptably activities). This is also true for the validation of the principle of moral individualism (that human beings are the only ones responsible for their actions and therefore must face the consequences on Judgment Day). Last but not least, the fact that

---

[3] To such an extent that the comparative studies between different Muslim religions today, from the angle of their sociological composition and more specifically the share of followers whose primary socialization, namely that which happens within the family during childhood, is done outside of a Muslim environment, show that Salafist communities are those standing out by the greatest number of people having embraced (and not inherited) Islam. The case of France shows a proportion of at least 30% according to a study I conducted in a number of French cities and regions (Adraoui 2020).

all ethnic origins are seen as equal and dissipate in Salafist universalism (for which only faith experienced as "orthodox" matters) provides this fundamentalist ethics with an important capacity to speak to and make sense to people who have been socialized in extremely different countries, and give it a strong potential for development.

THE SALAFIST ECONOMIC ETHICS: SALVATION BY WORLDLY SUCCESS?

While we saw above that the puritan revivalist episteme characterizing Salafism evokes forms of "Islamic Protestantism" where some doctrinal, cultural, or political phenomena are interpreted as deviations compared to the "authentic" last rites, another sphere—the economy—is useful for shedding light on other similarities with the protestant ethics. More specifically, comparisons can be made to the historical phase corresponding, according to Max Weber, to the emergence of modern capitalism at the dawn of the eighteenth century in Northern Europe (Weber 2004). Observers of Salafist communities almost all agree that there is a basic appeal for entrepreneurship, business, and social mobility. Being the partisans of a capitalist spirit that is steeped in morality and investment, many of these puritans value profit, and economic and financial independence, to the point of devaluing employment since it means depending on someone and not being able to conjugate rigorist aspirations and an appetite for business as well as certain forms of material possession. Still bound by the logics of moral distinction at the root of the Salafist approach, and which passes almost systematically by the conversion of transcendent religious principles into behavioral norms in the religious and social domains divided into "legal" and "illegal," the economy very much represents a sphere within which the logic of election finds all its meaning.

Max Weber detected in the system of values of Protestant communities established in various societies where the Reform had spread a body of attitudes enabling numerous affinities with the conditions of the emergence of modern capitalism, first of which is the primacy of savings over consumerism which explains accumulation of wealth followed by investment. The latter is certainly motivated by profit not by virtue of rational maximization behaviors, but rather the search for signs of divine approval. God, by granting success to the Protestant believer, announces a sign of his possible election, even while doubt remains. The Salafist ethics is characterized by certain similarities such as the desire to invest and become entrepreneurs/businessmen like a number of companions of Muḥammad in *Mekka* some fourteen centuries ago, known for its place in trade activity in the East (perfumes, slaves, spices, fabrics, etc.). Success in business as illustrated by the trajectories of a number of Western Salafists now linked to some Muslim countries by their creation of companies specialized in *ḥalāl* tourism (places where religious morality is respected such as the Island of Lombok in Indonesia) or in the pilgrimage to Saudi Arabia, or those of business owners in the *Derb Ghalef* neighborhood in Casablanca or some malls of the Sharjah emirate, is interpreted as the sign of divine approval, with a lower degree of anxiety that defines the protestant ethics according to Max Weber. To the contrary, as part of a symbolic rivalry with other branches of Islam, the profit-making purpose implied by the refusal to remain enslaved to salaried work (e.g., the intransigent practice unique to Salafism such as the need to conduct the five ritual prayers at specific times, preferably at the mosque) is interpreted as a proof of belonging to "the saved group." God thus appears to confirm the correct topographical choice by compensating "true" believers for their worldly and financial success on earth (permitting the enjoyment of material pleasures here as long as they are legal) in the expectation of eternal rewards beyond.

Salafism and Migration: The Case of *Hijra*

The *hijra*[4] is an ideal of a rupture to be achieved for followers embedded in a "land of infidels" who interpret their birth in a predominately non-Muslim context as an anomaly that exile is supposed to eliminate. Salafism here largely embodies a decentralized movement where, from one city to another, the connections between followers are not dense (the local level being the chosen space of socialization). Such a reality is even more visible in a Muslim-minority context.

---

[4] From the root h-j-r which refers to the departure, abandonment, or exile, in the image of the one undertaken in 622 by Muslims of *Mekka* toward *Madīna* in order to protect their faith. The obligation of leaving a land where the practice Islam is presented as threated is found in a number of contemporary *salafī* schools of thought.

The *hijra* cannot only be understood as the accomplishment of a necessary break up. This type of migration highlights a body of practices and subjectivities that make it possible to unveil certain symbolic forms of Salafism and to question the relationship that its followers have with their environment. The *hijra* demonstrates an "aesthetics" of existence, a certain relationship to a non-Muslim society, an idealization of the Islamic world, and a form of informal political engagement (even if quietist Salafists abhors organized activism), as well as a globalization of the margins operating both in the shadow of states and in opposition to them. By putting the focus on the *hijra*, and then resituating it in the unfolding of Salafist trajectories, it becomes possible to consider some of the global motivations of identifying with a certain contemporary fundamentalism.

The ethnography of the *hijra* leads to consider two founding logics of the Salafist dialectic in a Muslim-minority context. The first logic is related to status, since the followers, seeing themselves as contemporary embodiments of Islamic virtues, build an imaginary of superiority. Presenting themselves as the only Muslims capable of systematically abandoning a Western society for instance, in terms of both doctrine and practice, Salafists get involved *nolens volens* in a vertical relationship with the rest of society. The departure is idealized and interpreted as the result of the break up with "the domain of impiety[5]" *(dār al-kufr)* which represents, in the eyes of the followers, a practical and symbolic priority. The second founding logic is related to immunity since the capital of purity cannot be compromised by being immersed in the prevailing "depravation." The defensive and protective aim of the *hijra* echoes what can be referred to as a "Noah syndrome" (Adraoui 2020). Considering that the only salvation possible is found within a world and an era that are lost, these Salafists feel constrained to leave a geographic and symbolic space which carries off all those who were unable to escape it.

The Hijra in Salafism: The Fulfillment of "Allegiance and Disavowal"

The need to physically and morally split with "impiety" is rooted in the application of an essential principle in the Salafist narrative: "allegiance and disavowal" *(al-walā' wa al-barā')*. This is interpreted as a duty to

---

[5] Whose opposite is "the domain of Islam" *(dār al-islām)*.

swear allegiance to an idea or a social order that complies with the principle of divine unicity *(al-tawḥīd)* and to renounce those that betray it. This migration of salvation, such as it is expressed in Salafist communities, is part of this founding dichotomy between what "people of unicity" *(ahl al-tawḥīd)* call for and the context in which "the infidels" *(al-kuffār)*, as well as "deviant and lost" Muslims *(ahl al-bid'a wal-ḍalāla)*, live. Among the implications of the duty of allegiance and disavowal, the Saudi cleric Sālīḥ al-Fawzān (Al-Fawzān 1990) for instance cites not "living in countries [of non-Muslims], and not leaving them for a Muslim country in the aim of escaping to preserve one's religion."[6]

The imperative of allegiance and disavowal engenders a total relationship to the environment in the sense that every social interaction is interpreted through the lens of this necessity. The *hijra* comes to crystallize the highest level of rejection of non-Muslim society. Yet, exile is part of a gradual process, and the status of an emigrated Salafist *(al-muhājir)* is symbolically higher than that of followers who still lack enough self-confidence to leave for the East, the counter-image of the West for instance.

The *hijra* is a gradual process, made up of three steps. First, "internal" migration, which involves distancing oneself from the other by withdrawing socially into a "purified" living space. Then comes the "partial" or "temporary" migration, undertaken in the aim of socializing for a period in a Muslim country without definitively breaking with the country of origin. Finally comes the migration aimed at putting down roots in the "land of Islam," namely with the ultimate plan of renouncing prior citizenship and re-entering a genealogy that prior generations who migrated toward Western countries for example are deemed guilty of having altered.

The Internal Hijra: *Between Symbolic Withdrawal and the Premises of Departure*

As soon as the Salafist career is launched, the believer has the departure in mind in order to flee the moral "decadence" and political "animosity" directed toward Islam and Muslims. The media exposure of Salafism and "permissive" social changes are cited as the most legitimate reasons

---

[6] Sālīḥ al-Fawzān (born in 1933) is one of the eminent members and one of the most famous figures within the Committee of Great Scholars in Saudi Arabia.

for breaking up with non-Muslim society. The *hijra* in fact symbolizes two separations: the first is geographical, because outside of the historical sphere of Islam, the followers are not able to accept, within their perspective, the uprooting of prior generations who came to Europe for instance; the second is metaphysical, since the non-Islamic world is viewed as an avatar of moral antagonism that opposes "truth" and "lies." The two dimensions, status and immunity, are generally tightly interwoven in the process leading to the decision of leaving France where we can find an important Salafist community. For instance, a Salafist woman explains on a web site that she emigrated to Jordan for her children. While she felt "strong" enough to avoid enduring the "immorality" of France, she migrated so that her children could remain "pure" and "chaste," sheltered from a "pernicious" model of society that undermines the morality of believers as they integrate into it:

> If you are in France without children, I think it is possible to get by (if you forget that you always have to look at the ground in the street at the risk of running into a pole). But I don't feel capable of being the counterweight [sic] against French society when it comes to educating my children. I have a daughter and I don't see myself telling her "fear French law more than the law of Allāh" for the veil. I have a boy and I imagine it will be difficult for him not to look at girls and not to greet them with a kiss on the cheek at school. Where I am now (in Jordan), if my 4-year-old daughter wants to go out with the veil, I can let her without the fear of having the social services after me. I don't have the impression of saying to my children: in the house you have to act one way and outside another because in France religion is something so private that it must stay at home.[7]

Yet, even before the departure, the Salafist way of life is marked by a symbolic and practical renunciation, a form of anticipation of the external *hijra*; in sum, an internal migration. This echoes a geographical and moral restraint that is constantly being renewed. The structure of social networks and spaces of daily life, through the lens of allegiance and disavowal, provide a choice material for measuring the depth and intensity of this internal migration, synonymous first and foremost with a systematic withdrawal.

---

[7] http://la-hijra.over-blog.com/article-21512619.html [Accessed 11 November 2021].

The latter takes on three main forms. The first is geographical and expresses the religious rationalization of physical space. In this respect, the mosque becomes the main site of the Salafist counter-society by representing the physical and symbolic space of convergence of every moment of the puritan career. The imperative of purification and education *(al-taṣfiyya wal-tarbiyya)* that defines this way of life makes the mosque not only the privileged place of religious fulfillment, but also the heart of the counter-society that the followers are trying to build. Around the charismatic figure of the imam, who has the responsibility of spreading Salafist ideals and of establishing a focal point for identifying and building the norms of everyday life (marriage, education, religious practices, etc.), the Salafist communities construct a symbolic and physical barricade between themselves and the other. Social life comes to be built around the necessity of being close to the mosque, due to the possibilities for moral purification that it represents. While waiting to definitively seek exile in order to live their religion "without shame," Salafists constantly redefine the shape of this internal *hijra*, which represents the step preceding the big departure. Combining moral considerations and physical constraints, they practice on a daily basis an ethics of preservation and withdrawal which occurs notably by ceasing to spend time in spaces that are mixed, or where Muslim presence is small, or where "decadent" culture is manifested.

The second form taken is the reduction of the social network to a group of fellows by the establishment of strict matrimonial and familial strategies. The persistence of the Noah syndrome, combined with the "saved group" ethics, pushes Salafists to make the acquired "purity" long-lasting by projecting themselves in an "orthodox" genealogy, of which the family cell is the first link. The mosque, the imam, and networks of religious peers are thus mobilized at the time of matrimonial union. Finally, as we previously saw, maternity is often the factor immediately triggering the external *hijra*. Indeed, becoming a parent concretely triggers the movement toward exile since it becomes a question of making the split with French society durable over the long term. If "Salafist spaces" exist around the mosques of some cities, the basic trend is still to valorize the Muslim East, the only place able to propose a definitive break up with the "impious" environment.

Finally, the third form reflects a growing Orientalization of one's lifestyle, imaginary, and language. Knowledge of "Islamic civilization" serves as a basis for moral and religious purification: the daily life of believers is structured around cultural references specific to Muslim countries, and more specifically those of the Gulf societies which are the most strongly valued due to their supposed faithfulness to Islamic orthodoxy. Clothing (the full veil, *qamīṣ*, etc.), education (the prestige of Saudi Islamic universities and Yemenite, Egyptian, or Jordanian religious centers for instance), and models of society (a synthesis of capitalism and religion) are all essentialized elements that serve as a model for numerous Salafists. It is thus not surprising that the large majority of the followers we may encounter mention Saudi Arabia, the United Arab Emirates, or Yemen (before the war) as chosen destinations for conducting their *hijra*.

The Short-Term Hijra: *A First Step Toward a Final Break*

Most often, the final departure is not the first contact with the "land of Islam." Indeed, the *hijra*, as a Salafist learning process, is made up of a series of encounters and stays with Eastern Islamic societies prior to the final migration. A number of Salafists carry out intermediary, short trips, similar to those undertaken by European students who go for a time to study outside of their home country so as to combine university studies with cultural exploration. If, unlike *Erasmus* students, European Salafists want to break up with their country permanently, it is interesting to make the parallel between the two processes. While European Salafists have a preference for the country of origin of their families who settled in Europe when it was a question of putting down roots somewhere else, in order to make a final break up with Western "impiety," for their "learning process" they instead seek out societies to which they have no attachments. Egypt is a good example, even if since the revolution of 2011, and the authoritarian turn in 2013, the Egyptian government is drastically opposed to the settlement of foreigners, even temporarily, in the country. Up until recent years, over 700 French Salafists have for instance visited there, Cairo primarily, for short periods, generally one year at most, in order to become familiar with Islam as a major cultural fact. This prerequisite to the final *hijra* is above all motivated by a personal project of religious training through the mobilization of local and global Salafist networks. The Salafists go to Egypt to register with the *al-Azhar* university, or a less prestigious institution that is still popular, such as the *Ibāna* Center located in the *Madīnat al-Nasr* neighborhood (not far from one of the main streets of Cairo, the *Makram al-ʿAbīd* avenue). Founded in the 1990s by American Salafists, the *Ibāna* Center welcomes a large majority of Westerners who have come to learn Arabic and Islamic sciences (Quranic study, history of the Prophets, law, etc.). The profiles are almost always the same: French Salafist Muslims living in the *banlieues*—a number of which are married and have children (the trip is most often with the family)—who have come not only for the prestige of the country within the Islamic imaginary, but also, more practically, due to its easy access for European citizens (at least until the revolution). At the intersection of the local identity of Salafists from Western societies, advised and guided by former pioneers, and a transnational context where Salafists join the entire world to share a same conception of dogma and existence, this form of *hijra* participates considerably in building a shared ethic that is only solidified intermittently on a given place. The existence of these essential spaces of learning and training (whether it be a religious space in a Western country or a globalized Cairo religious center) plays a key role in "emotional community spirit" (Rosenwein 2006).

The primary figure of the Salafist who migrated to Egypt is that of a student who went to seek a puritan religious education that doesn't exist in the West (despite the growing possibility of creating spaces of "purity" in certain religious sites dedicated to an "orthodox" vision). The *hijra*, in this case, gives rise to a story of learning which ties together a student's experience with immersion in a society that is historically marked by Islam.

The Final Hijra*: Completion of the Rupture?*

The final migration represents the completion of the return to "orthodoxy" that the Salafist career is supposed to represent. Indeed, it depicts the end of the trajectory of separation that is the aim and means of the Salafist ideal. It embodies, in a certain way, the totality of the rupture with a Muslim-minority context, as, theoretically, it is after this final migration that the Western Salafist ideal takes its full shape, placing the believer in the image of an irreversible trajectory. While Egypt becomes less and less accessible, European Salafists are choosing the country of origin of their parents as a final destination. Given that followers of Algerian origin are a majority within these communities, Algeria for instance is the main destination for French candidates of the *hijra* who want to split with France. As a process of rediscovering one's origins (which cannot be considered as exclusive to Salafists, or even to Muslims), the *hijra* embodies a radical reorientation of the way of living and the meaning of existence. The candidate of this final migration seeks, at least theoretically, to erase traces of their former socialization and to repair damage caused by "deviance" (both moral and geographical) that was initiated by past generations who left their country of origin to finally "get lost" in the "land of impiety." If the past years have seen a true diversification in terms of migration destinations toward "new" countries—where the promise of economic growth and possibilities of personal success appear attractive for Salafists often characterized, despite the undeniable success of some, by impoverishment and relegation in Europe (United Arab Emirates, Malaysia, etc.)—the family country of origin remains a chosen destination for completing the abandonment of Europe.

If the *hijra* is motivated by an important symbolic dimension (returning toward the past by regaining "the land of authenticity"), candidates of final migration often choose to settle in the country of origin of their parents because it is easier to mobilize private resources, notably from the family. In Algiers, for instance, almost all Salafists we can meet live in the home of their parents who, for their part, still live on the other side of the Mediterranean Sea. The logic is substantially different from short-term migration in that, once settled, the Salafist redefines their puritan religious practice on a daily basis as part of a "classical" familial existence, without a militant or political aspect to the practice (since the hypothetical obstacles of a non-Islamic culture have been lifted). They remain faithful to the necessity of remaining removed from spheres of power. It is especially important to continue to rise up against co-religionists who are not initiated to "orthodoxy," while shielding themselves against the torments of an era "in perdition." The priority, once settled in "the land of Islam," resides in reinforcing religious education as well as worldly success (the importance of social and economic mobility).

If the final *hijra* naturally implies continuing the duty of religious training, the emigrant must now focus on survival and economic well-being, as moving to a country, even if it is their country of familial origin, does not necessarily ensure better material conditions. Given the fact that cultural combat is easier once "the land of Islam" has been reached, other considerations emerge as they establish roots. Personal and family networks are thus used to obtain loans (outside of the official banking system operating on the principle of usury called *ribā'*), or for gaining access to certain clienteles adapted to the nature of their business (food services, moving services, taxis, etc.). The figure of the pious entrepreneur embodies the Salafist experience of final migration. The mosque remains a chief space of socialization, but the Islamic reputation of the country matters less than the material conditions of existence: proximity of a familial network, the possibility of regularly returning to Europe, or even relative political stability are all elements that are taken into account in the development of a migratory strategy. While the imperfections of the Algerian system (corruption, nepotism, inequalities, etc.) are not denied, the moral and cultural argument against life in the West prevails.

In short, the study of the *hijra* in Muslim-minority countries makes it possible to shed light on a broader body of symbols and counter-symbols by virtue of which these puritan communities implement a project of total separation with a despised model of society. The emphasis on the desire to migrate for salvation among Salafists corresponds, in terms of both the aim and the strategies implemented, to an original double phenomenon of extraversion/withdrawal. Among the numerous traits of the *hijra*, these two dynamics are indeed interesting in that they make it possible to see the Salafist ethic of otherness as at once a local and globalized phenomenon. Analyzed from this ethnographic point of view, the essential practice of this hardline religiosity makes it possible to depict a threefold crisis. First, a crisis of the Western model, since the values on display no longer seem to have a hold over a certain number of actors who are symbolically and territorially marginalized by the way society actually works. A crisis of the state, secondly, to the extent that the most intense phenomena of personal and collective identity are no longer observed at the state-national level but at the local and transnational levels. Salafists embody a textbook case of a U-shaped identity formation (namely, a strong feeling of social belonging at the neighborhood level as well as to co-religionists at the global level, but a weak identification with fellow Western citizens)—an identity formation which is moreover the case among a number of minorities. Finally, a crisis of integration, the most obvious, which the project of total separation that is sought in the completion of the *hijra* makes highly emblematic. Understood as the opposite path taken by past generations, who wished to settle north of the Mediterranean, the *hijra* embodies in this regard more than ever a counter-migration that is religiously motivated and reflects the difficulty felt by certain Muslims to complete the life change desired by their predecessors several decades ago.

References

Adraoui, M.A. 2020. *Salafism Goes Global: From the Gulf to the French Banlieues*. New York: Oxford University Press.

Al-Fawzān, S. 1990. *Al-walā' wa al-barā'*. JIMAS.

Ismail, R. 2021. *Rethinking Salafism: The Transnational Networks of Salafi 'Ulama in Egypt, Kuwait, and Saudi Arabia*. New York, NY: Oxford University Press.

Mouline, N. 2014. *The Clerics of Islam: Religious Authority and Political Power in Saudi Arabia*. New Haven, CT: Yale University Press.

Rosenwein, B.H. 2006. *Emotional Communities in the Early Middle Ages*. Ithaca Press.

Roy, O. 2014. *The Holy Ignorance: When Religion and Culture Part Ways*. New York, NY: Columbia University Press.

Weber, M. 2004. *The Protestant Ethic and the "Spirit" of Capitalism*. Penguin Books.

CHAPTER 8

Understanding Past and Today Jihadism

Abstract This section focuses on the issue of jihadism and attempts to put into perspective the evolutions and mutations that have characterized this ideology for several decades. By focusing on the main transformations brought about in the history of jihadism by the project linked to the Islamic State Organization, this chapter highlights the possible emergence of a new Jihadist ethic potentially disconnected from any direct Salafist heritage.

Keywords Caliphate State · Terrorist Attacks · Jihadist Radicalization · Middle Eastern Conflicts · Syria/Iraq

From *Jihād* to Jihadism

Armed Jihād *Between Historical Exception and Today Systematization*

Based on the Arabic root j-h-d, the concept of *jihād* in the Muslim religion refers to the effort undertaken in order to change the state of a person or a group toward a greater degree of moral, spiritual, social, and sometimes legal allegiance to Islam. It designates a positive action whose aim is to achieve compliance with the spirit and the text (although widely debated) of the Tradition. This notion, central in the different historical forms adopted by Islam, is thus deeply tied to the aims of believers, who are a part of various social configurations by virtue of which they assess specific priorities. It is therefore not only a concept with multiple meanings, but also importantly one that can be stretched and extended, in that the aspiration toward a more Islamic existence can potentially concern all spheres of human life. The scope, the activity, the methodology, and the aims of *jihād* thus form what we refer to as the core founding issues of Jihadism. Through these dimensions, it becomes possible to grasp the imaginary of actors of radicalization in various contexts where it has been observed for a number of years.

Unlike radical integralist movements, which aim to transform their societies without using strategies of physical violence, and without forgetting the majority of believers who favor a pacifist conception of this effort for God, Jihadist movements have been for several decades updating religious debates with the aim of legitimizing contemporary antagonisms with regard to a series of various enemies, who are united, in the Jihadist perspective, by their animosity toward "authentic" Islam. In this way, the current phenomena of political and religious violence using reference to Islam claim to be part of a specific religious imaginary, that of armed *jihād* (Turner 2014) as it has been understood for several centuries in *sunnī* tradition.

The first space or dimension related to this ideological mold is that of the enemy and thus refers to the doctrinal perimeter of adversity, the past and present definition of which makes it possible to speak of a switch from *jihād* to Jihadism. Unlike historically dominant interpretations within the *fiqh al-jihād* ("understanding of *jihad*") that are not based on the figure of the enemy in the modern sense of the word,[1] contemporary Jihadist movements put this at the heart of their engagement. Their ideological transformation of religion is thus primarily carried out by constructing an imaginary that is grounded in ontological enmity. It is because certain groups are presented as extreme toward Muslims that Jihadist thinkers and militants consider themselves justified to declare a form of martial law against them. Historically, this responsibility of

---

[1] It is indeed primarily a question of the short-term adversary. If the defense of the *umma* is a constant in all theories regarding the right to use force, there is no specific and constant definition of the antagonistic figure. It is the responsibility of the clergy to define the enemy within a specific context, how to fight him, and for what exact purposes.

defending "Islam/Muslims in danger" mainly fell on political powers claiming, in a wide range of regimes (caliphates, sultanates, emirates, kingdoms and more recently presidential systems, etc.), to represent all or part of the *umma*. It is thus primarily a question of a defensive *jihād* whose mission is to re-establish a power that draws its legitimacy from religious belonging and respect of Islamic orders, be these legal, moral, jurisdictional, or cultural, in the absence of which the practice of the Muslim religion would be threatened. In other words, because it ensures the continuation of the practice of Islam as a religion, armed combat is legitimate (Cook 2005; Aboud El Fadl 1999; Abou El Fadl 2001).

Since the nature of the opposition that is supposed to unite, from this perspective, Muslims against otherness is no longer purely metaphysical or religious but also political and conflictual, the principles declared in normal times become suspended, as authorized by Islamic clerics who have proposed to conceptualize the *fiqh al-jihād* for centuries (Bonney 2004). These clerics have rendered violence and even killing lawful and feasible because the *umma* is in a situation of war, meaning that what is usually professed must give way to a logic of exception. If, for instance, peace is the norm, the advent of an exceptional situation authorizing all or some Muslims to reason in terms of necessity *(al-ḍarūra)* renders the use of force not only advisable but necessary in order to combat adversity (Peters 1996). This martial construction of politics on behalf of a religious framing of the Islamic individual and collective needs raises essential questions for researchers, who must then consider Jihadism as the systematization of martial law from which specific issues emerge.

The Contemporary Origins of Jihadism

At the crossroads of Jihadism,[2] we have two schools of thought which have interacted to produce the conception of armed combat that leads us to talk about Jihadism today. The evolution of militant, political, and radicalized Islam in the twentieth century gave birth to a new vision, one that certainly inherits the traits of previous centuries, but which also projects itself in a new symbolic and military space.

The evolution of Egyptian Muslim Brotherhood is a first key factor. This movement was first concerned with preaching at the time of

---

[2] Which is then nothing but a modern ideology in itself, making it irrelevant to mention a "past" nor "contemporary" type of Jihadism.

its founder, Hasan Al-Bannā' (1906-assassinated in 1949) (Lia 1999). However, the movement's ideology gave birth to, via the radical(ized) thinker Sayyid Qutb (1906-executed in 1966) (Calvert 2010), a vision that adopts the early fundamentalist heritage but disqualifies, once pushed to its extreme, the military regime at the head of the Egyptian state since the July 1952 *Coup d'état* that brought Jamal ʿAbd al-Nāsir and the *Free Officers Movement* to power. The radicalization of the Brotherhood's thought was first carried out against an authority that was guilty, in the eyes of a number of increasingly violent activists from the 1970s onwards, of usurping identification with Islam even though its actions were supposed to show the contrary (the hunting down of Islamists being in their eyes a sign of disloyalty). This is why the notion of *jihād* was reactivated by the first "Islamic groups" *(al-jamāʿāt al-islāmiyya)* that began to theorize the right to violence (against a regime that "betrays" Islam). Armed *jihād* against "the deviant prince," and by extension against its allies, was thus integrated into the customs of Islamic movements, subsequently forming part of the contemporary conception of Jihadism (Kepel 2003b).

The second source of influence comes from the Arabian Peninsula by virtue of the strengthening and globalization of Salafist theses (as mainly expressed in the *wahhābī* doctrinal, political, and historical experience within the Saudi context). Indeed, the understanding of the dogma and social relations taught in the years of the Islamist consensus in Saudi Arabia (benefiting from its energetic centrality following the second half of the twentieth century) also participates in the emergence of a Jihadist landscape. While contemporary Salafism (Meijer 2009; Cavatorta and Merone 2017) is marked by intense debates, which aim to revive original Islam,[3] it cannot be denied that the schools of thought that are prone toward a systematized armed *jihād* were influenced by the fundamentalism taught within the oil monarchies. Reflecting the image of the religious and military struggle borne in the eighteenth century following the alliance between the imam Muḥammad b. Abd al-Wahhāb and the tribal leader Muḥammad b. Saʿūd (Al-Rasheed 2010), some Jihadist movements perpetuated this armed *jihād* for "authentic" Islam. The war in Afghanistan during the 1980s thus enabled generations of fighters from

---

[3] See Chapters 1, 4 and 5.

the Muslim world (and beyond) to come to this country in order to lead the first armed *jihād* at a global level.

A breaking point is observed after this period as several generations of armed *jihād* actors started affirming that the liberation of the Islamic Afghan territory was only one step in the struggle for the re-establishment of the *umma*'s rights that have been "scorned." The ambition, no longer only circumstantial but, from then on, pan-Islamic and unspecified at a geographic and temporal level (any situation turning to the disadvantage of Muslims could be targeted by armed *jihād*), turned the first movements of defense of Muslim communities into a model to follow during broader conflicts to come. The convergence of different generations of radicalized actors who began to redirect their engagement toward an aim detached from any specific territories to the benefit of an "opportunistic" struggle is a central phenomenon. The theater of action will now depend on conflicts occurring in Muslim societies, even if the fuse was not lit by any initial religious representation (Chechnya, Bosnia, Iraq, Syria, Mali, etc.). This led to the a posteriori justification of armed *jihād* in order to mobilize co-religionists in the name of a sacred reference against authorities who were blamed for usurping Islamic belonging (the Saudi monarchy after the Gulf War, the Egyptian military regime, the Syrian *baʿthī* state ruled by *shīʿa*[4] leaders, etc.) and against which is pronounced the anathema *(al-takfīr)*. This subsequently makes it legal to overthrow a power that is no longer Muslim, while leading the fight against the powers accused of weaving a conspiracy against the *umma*. It is through this opposition strategy that armed *jihād* became the regulating factor of Islamic identity among several radical groups in the last several decades. The relation to otherness thus constitutes the trademark of the Jihadist experience (Roy 2017).

The Core Questions in Jihadism

Who is the Enemy?

Jihadism distinguishes itself by ignoring customary laws that correspond to periods of peace, thus justifying the use of force and more generally

---

[4] *Shīʿa* Muslims being one of the most detested groups among Jihadist. The latter even call them *rawāfiḍ* ("renegades") for "violating" early Islam's principles and attitudes in discrediting some of Muḥammad's most eminent companions for instance.

the suspension of all or part of daily customs and practices (e.g., the right to no longer pray in defense of the city if the enemy is at its walls, etc.). It also stands apart from the vision that is generally described as "classic" armed *jihād* (*jihād bi-l-sayf*[5]) by its global stance. The latter no longer consists of restricting the military effort to a given territory or political configuration, but in igniting a world revolution with the aim of producing a sole and exclusive sovereignty commanding the entire *umma*. If the theme of defending co-religionists remains central, as illustrated by the conflict in Afghanistan, it is now through a form of global insurrection, not bound to a specific territory (at least until the emergence of the Islamic State Organization[6]), and no longer to a geographically situated struggle, that the Jihadist vanguard aims to unite the *umma* (Holbrook 2014).

Then, the first issue of Jihadism concerns the perimeter of adversity and, by extending the ideological and military target, the first imperative becomes naming the enemy (Schmitt 2007). The enemy is the one opposed to the promotion of "authentic" Islam, the defense of which is ensured by believers who are lucid and determined enough to handle this responsibility. This means, therefore, that since the "unimpaired" Islam for which Jihadists fight is subsequently faith and nation, dogma and territory, law and sovereignty, the figure of the enemy is extendible and able to evolve. Here resides the first impetus of the phenomena of radicalization, since it consists in the triggering of violence with the aim of achieving a specific strategic objective and/or generating psychological terror aimed to weaken the enemy.

If, until the 1990s, Jihadist commitment was carried out in reaction to two main figures of injustice, the last decade of the twentieth century witnessed some major changes that now structure the landscape of violence, more dynamic and disparate than ever before. Until this period, Jihadist targets were essentially States that "betrayed" Islam. One famous example of this is the Egyptian regime as evidenced by the wave of attacks against military bases in the country and charges against leading political dignitaries, namely President Anwār al-Sādāt (1918–1981) who was assassinated over a military parade celebrating the 1973 war against

---

[5] "*Jihād* through the sword".

[6] *Daesh* as an acronym of *dawla al-islāmiyya fi-l-'irāq wa-bilād al-shām* ('the Islamic State in Iraq and the Levant').

Israel by some members of the Egyptian Islamic group *Jihād* led by Khālid al-Islambūlī (1955–1982). Later on, non-Muslim states started to be targeted by armed *jihād* with a view to liberating conquered Muslim territory like with Afghanistan in the 1980s yet initially through a strict territorial agenda that was limited to the land to be liberated on behalf of Islam (not nationalism). Current Jihadism stands apart by its broader and deeper space of adversity.

The 1990s largely signaled the current evolutions influencing phenomena of today Jihadist radicalization. Since this time, the extensiveness of the space of adversity has produced, under the notable influence of the Algerian conflict and the first globalized wave of *al-Qāʿida* Jihadism (Kepel 2003a), an increasingly demilitarized conceptualization of the enemy.[7] If the actors of contemporary armed *jihād* see themselves as soldiers, their targets must theoretically be part of a martial relationship, which means that the enemy represents an *alter ego* and must be the paradigmatic target within this perspective. Yet this space of Jihadism has subsequently undergone an important break, as the religious construction that presides over this engagement starts to include civilians as part of an ideological and opportunistic gradation involving both military personnel of targeted states and people removed from the military apparatus but regarded as statutorily or morally united with these states.

If the conflict in Afghanistan evidenced a relatively classic military opposition between two camps (the Soviet army and its local allies on the one hand and anti-regime forces assisted in particular by the first transnational Jihadist communities on the other[8]), Russian civilians were for instance never targeted. The martial law of the period confined the use of violence to a bilateral antagonism in which the enemies were both clearly

---

[7] The Algerian conflict of the 1990s, also defined by some as a real civil war, saw the military regime and armed Islamist forces clash in the wake of the cancelled legislative elections of December 1991, which had seen a very large victory for the Islamic Salvation Front, the main Islamic party since the late 1980s. Many Algerians who had served in the conflict in Afghanistan participated in the building of the ISF once they returned to their country, feeding the opposition to the regime that emerged from independence of an Islamist camp whose "stolen victory" in the early 1990s will precipitate the country into a bloody civil war where Islamist armed forces such as the *Islamic Salvation Army* and the even more radical *Armed Islamic Group* (Martinez 2000) will stand out, from which a significant part of the formations that have pledged allegiance in Algeria and the Maghreb to *al-Qāʿida* and even to the Islamic State, have emerged today.

[8] Even though they practically did not fight.

identified and territorialized. The extensiveness of armed *jihād* was weak back then, but it substantially evolved a decade later when the identification of an Algerian "usurping state" influenced a domestic battle, which was no longer against an "invader of the land of Islam" but rather against a "treacherous" power. The considerations that followed concerned the definition of hostility that Algerian Jihadist groups confronted. Primarily, this included the *Islamic Salvation Army* (a direct emanation of the political movement *Islamic Salvation Front*) and the *Armed Islamic Group* (more radical and at odds with the "minimalist" strategy of the former since it targeted, beyond the military, any individual or group accused of coming to its aid or defending its actions). Are people who do not serve in the military but who work for the state, such as police officers, legitimate targets? What about the families of these individuals? Is it right to expand the space of Jihadism even if it means throwing society into a full insurrection? The Algerian conflict is even more important as it heralds, in its French component, the junction between a national and international agenda that has become central in today's Jihadist movements. If much still needs to be clarified about the interconnected ties and instrumentations between certain Jihadist groups and the Algerian regime of the period (Martinez 2000), France, as a country accused of supporting the government of the time, became a legitimate target. French civilians were at risk of a violent attack at any moment by, for instance, inside fighters like Khaled Kelkal,[9] whose story has common elements with a number of current traits of terrorist radicalization phenomena (prior involvement in "classic" criminality networks, a history of weak religious practice, and the weight of familial and social deculturation) (Roy 2017).

The same debates can be observed within *al-Qāʿida* during this time. It was at this time that the first de-territorialized attacks were organized by the true first global Jihadist movement, fueled by a consideration of the enemy as encompassing not only opposing armies but all persons linked with a group identified as hostile toward Muslims, to the point of integrating the geographic territory of non-Muslim power into the scope of violent action. Thus, after having proclaimed the Soviet Union defeated by its attacks, the first generations of armed combat for Islam turn against the United States. The United States was accused not only of sponsoring the Israeli State for decades, but also of supporting incumbent regimes

---

[9] The perpetrator of the attacks in the Saint-Michel train station on July 25, 1995, was linked to the *Armed Islamic Group* and killed by the French police while at large.

in the Muslim world that were actually "treacherous" for being politically and strategically involved in alliances that harmed the Islamic *umma*, as for instance illustrated by the proximity maintained for several decades between Saudi Arabia and the United States. With the aim to expel the American ally from Islamic territory and more specifically from the Arabian Peninsula, *al-Qāʿida* (Gerges 2011), through the intermediary of Usāma b. Lāden (1957–2011), designated military targets as a priority (in the context of an identified conflict to which was added a Jihadist force or a terrorist enterprise aimed to influence the morale or political orientation of the enemy). The attacks of September 11, 2001, on U.S. territory (foreshadowed by a first attack in 1993, the targeting of American embassies in Kenya as well as in Tanzania in 1998, and the offensive against the USS Cole in the Gulf of Aden on October 12, 2000), as well as military and terrorist Jihadist movements in Iraq after 2003 against the American invasion, but also the *shīʿa* presence (strengthened by the fall of Saddam Hussein), form part of a war built ideologically from the identification of a double enemy. This enemy is imagined in the two images of the invader and the traitor (or the usurper). In this respect, faithful to a martial conception of the legal foundations on which the *fiqh al-jihād* is based, if civilians are killed during a conflict or act of terrorism, they are considered—even if they are "good Muslims"—collateral victims whose death is unavoidable. This is because the good (the defense of the *umma*) resulting from their death is seen as greater than the distress caused to individuals and their families.

The political and religious configuration of this period, despite notable changes, breaks with the current generation, which is not only involved in a phenomenon of re-territorialization of the Jihadist project, but maybe above all in an explosion of the space of adversity. A Jihadist paradigm shift has been initiated by the Islamic State by virtue of which the *umma* is now supposed to have its own state (Gerges 2017). The relationship with the rest of the world conditions a permanent state of war (Hashim 2017) in the aim of encompassing by force over the long term all of Muslim territory, and even potentially more. Thus, the caliphate-immediate building principle (Wasserstein 2017) led to a central ideological reformation within Jihadist movements. With geographic expansionism clearly at the core of their ambition, a constant state of conflict is created with an incessantly growing number of enemies, the number of which but also the nature of which is subject to constant fluctuation in order to justify the constant movement on which the Islamic

State[10] was founded. All the states which ended up intervening in the Syrian (or Iraqi-Syrian) conflict, taking into account the involvement of the Islamic State, are likely to be identified as enemies of Islam, and no longer just because they are found guilty of being allies of "corrupt" regimes or nations at war against Muslims (Israel for instance). Stepping in front of the path of the "State of the Caliphate/Caliphate State" means war, and hostility toward powers like France, the United States, and Russia is no longer motivated by them having assisted discredited regimes in the Muslim world, but rather by their direct military intervention against modern Jihadist movements.[11]

Such a change has clear repercussions on phenomena of radicalization within predominately Muslim societies but also beyond, as radicalization now has two main faces, unlike what happened with movements linked to *al-Qāʿida* (Staffel and Awan 2016). First, joining a conflict zone where the Islamic State is involved no longer has the sole objective of bringing down a specific enemy but of gaining an expanding embryonic state. In other words, armed *jihād* and *hijra* are now combined. Second, the permanent state of war for people who identify themselves in this project, but remain in their country, produces an imported type of conflict. This conflict corresponds to a low-intensity struggle that feeds itself on ideological allegiances that are now transnational, but especially on a quest for "savagery"[12] whereby moral weakening becomes at least as important as

---

[10] The slogan of which is in this sense is explicit: "Stay and spread up" *(bāqiyya wa-tatamaddad)*.

[11] This is illustrated by a famous text from the 1990s by Ayman Al-Zawāhirī (1951–2022) aimed against the Egyptian Muslim Brotherhood. There is no longer any way to solve the huge problems of the Muslim world except through violence and armed *jihād* with a view to re-establishing the Caliphate in the long-term, legal Islamist engagement having only sparked a "bitter harvest" (Hatina 2012).

[12] As shown by the text of the theorist (whose identity is on doubt) Abū Bakr al-Nājī, *The Administration of Savagery: The Most Critical Stage through which the Umma will Pass*, published online in 2004. This book discusses the need to provoke military interventions in enemy states in order to widen recruitment opportunities among co-religionists living in these countries. According to this text, the Islamic State could influence with its propaganda by structuring in an enduring way a divide within societies that have remained for a long time aside from conflicts involving Jihadist forces. This text grants central importance to the administration of an extreme level and type of brutality *(idārat al-tawaḥush)* with the aim of making an impression, but also of putting the enemy at fault by pushing it in turn toward the worst systematic violence against Muslims.

human and material destruction. The effect of stupefaction and omnipotence, particularly in a primarily non-Muslim context, leads to diversifying the figure of the enemy, even to totalizing it, by seeking to target the security of an entire social body, and no longer a specific objective. As such, the enemy is not only the state but also the society that is supposed to produce the anti-Islamic policies against which Jihadists intend to react.

Since, unlike *al-Qāʿida*, the targets are indiscriminate, the sociological profile of the attacks of the last several years has been characterized by a different kind of violent opportunism. A form of inventiveness is left to the actor, who is no longer in this context a fighter of armed *jihād* only but rather a "soldier of the Caliphate" (Manne 2017), meaning that their actions must serve the propaganda and strategy of a state seeking permanent war. The two main categories of enemies have thus become holders or representatives of a sovereign function or authority. This is illustrated by the murder of two French police officers committed by Larossi Abballa in the city of Magny-en-Vexin in 2016, the attack against British soldiers in London in 2017, or the killing of a regular individual which is mainly motivated by inflicting psychological terror (even if the strategic agenda is never absent). In this latter case, the question no longer involves collateral victims, but rather primary targets and these attacks are not the result of an initial combat between military forces or institutional security services (army, police, etc.), but conceived to impose the idea of a cross-cutting conflict led against any person or group deemed worthy of being killed. Armed *jihād* is in this sense an individualized process where a person or a small network first conceives of their radicalization before theorizing about a target, unlike previous generations that became radicalized because they already had an enemy in mind (the United States, Arab regimes, etc.). The definition of the target is thus more individualized and in a certain way part of the "biography" of the fighter-soldier who will find people to violently attack. If the overall cognitive framework is provided by the imaginary promoted by the Islamic State, the individual aspect is essential. The latter enables a psychologically rooted Jihadism, to the extent that the target is only rarely specified in an ideological supra-discourse, to the benefit of individual creativity bearing on both the mode of action and the potential victim.

Moreover, the Islamic State generation, which developed outside of the Muslim world, distinguishes itself by the search for a homology between its targets and the groups fought by the caliphate in the Middle East. The opposition henceforth concerns any representative of a group against which the Caliphate State is built, such as Christian minorities in Syria and Iraq, with fighters of the Jihadist movement called to target the same groups in Europe as well. This explains, for example, the beheading of Father Jacques Hamel in Saint-Étienne-du-Rouvray on July 26, 2016, in the same way as the enemies of the Islamic State in the Middle East. In this respect, unlike the process of defining the enemy within *al-Qāʿida*-affiliated groups, there does not seem to be a separation between "the close enemy" ("fake" Muslim regimes) and "the far enemy" (non-Muslim states coming to their aid, primarily the United States) (Gerges 2009). This is because the state-building process that characterizes the Islamic State, as well as its expansionist aim, generates a field of adversity that is all over the place. Soldiers, civilians, and religious individuals are all metaphysical, political, and strategic enemies that justify a shift in the fighting paradigm used by actors in the wake of the Islamic State.

Who Must Lead Jihād *and Jihadism?*

The issue of conducting armed *jihād* follows a similar rationale of expansion and diversification. Indeed, it seems today that the deterritorialization that has been advocated for several decades by *al-Qāʿida*, as well as the attempt to build an Islamic state in the Middle East before envisioning its geographic expansion, generated a globalized identification with the Jihadist agenda. It is no longer only a question of rushing to defend a threatened religion, but also of taking part in a utopic plan, even seeking death rather than defending co-religionists. Therein lies a kind of reversal of the historical logic present in works dealing with armed *jihād*, since coming to the help of fellow Muslims remains important but gives rise to a desire for omnipotence specific to contemporary Jihadism. We can clearly see it in the experience led by "the State of the Caliphate/Caliphate State" (i.e., the Islamic State). The gain previously expected was moral, measured by the yardstick of divine approval. It is today palpable because it is indexed on the success of a new type of state construction. It is no longer only a question of coming to aid but of radically changing the terms of the political and religious authority in Muslim territory. The meaning of defending the interests of the *umma* has thus dramatically changed. The individualism of the approach and the motivation is seen in the way that victims are secondary. A number of fighters have nonetheless demanded to take part in the Syrian conflict or to carry out attacks in their countries against enemies that are targeted according to a rationale that is increasingly diluted and extensive. It is thus no longer a question of leading a religious and military effort with the aim of re-establishing all or part of the *umma* with well-understood rights (security, dignity, etc.). Instead, it involves fulfilling oneself through military Jihad as well as through the participation in a project that is not only defensive but also one that seeks to overthrow all previously observed states and social structures. Thus, the Jihadist engagement evokes a profound change in the way the armed fight for Islam is conducted.

The two main categories of believers are historically in charge of the theorization as well as the implementation of armed *jihād*. Between these two categories, only one is indisputably involved in this military effort, notwithstanding the time and place. The second is interpreted by the first with regard to the depth and nature of its involvement.

The first group is the Islamic clerics, who for a number of centuries were distinguishable by their function of managing the goods of salvation intended for their co-religionists. Most often, they interact with a political authority, which they offer to guide toward greater compliance of religious principles (which is in this sense a method also thought of as *jihād* through good advice). The orthodox position defended by the majority of clerics (mainly from the *sunnī* branch for centuries) is consented obedience. In other words, society, understood as a political sphere, is made up of three types of actors, only two of which have the freedom to hold power in theory. Due to a fear of anarchy and revolt *(al-fitna)*, which is constitutive of the political order in this perspective, the people must focus on spiritual and worldly affairs in such a way as to reserve the responsibility of power to clerics and princes. Clerics, drawing their legitimacy from their mastery of the sacred texts, legitimize the princes, who are in turn forced in their exercise of power to comply with religious orders (absence of moral perversion, defense of the *umma*, respect of prescriptions contained the *sharī'a* (Amanat and Griffel 2007), etc.). Thus, clerics hold a bi-polar position within Muslim society, in the interaction between the people and the princes, while ensuring to provide the latter with the demands of the former (justice, protection, morality, etc.), in exchange for the people's obedience to the prince. Yet, this religious construction contains in itself the possible reason for a dispute. What is the status of deviation from or even of an apparent or proven betrayal by the prince with regard to Islam such as it is defended by the clergy who have nonetheless legitimized the incumbent power? Do the people, who have been asked to obey in order to bring about the conditions of religious and political stability, now have the right to break the agreed constraint of allegiance (Wagemakers 2012a)?[13]

It is now possible to understand why the role of conducting armed *jihād* falls into two categories of actors within this vision. When the enemy is in this way internal, clerics who have not betrayed the *umma*, as well as the segments of people who follow them, are authorized to declare armed *jihād* against the deviant prince, whose self-declared belonging to Islam does not suffice to justify the allegiance because their actions are interpreted as antagonistic to the religious order. The reform for exercising power no longer happens through the intervention of the clergy cooperating on good terms with the prince toward greater compliance with religious norms and values. Instead, it is exercised by a violent military movement undertaken with the aim of pushing the holder of political authority back to greater Islamic reason, or even more radically, of removing the power in favor of a new authority that is supposedly faithful to the Islamic order. When the enemy is external, the ordinary clergy-believer duo must act in order to protect the political and social body that the *umma* represents from a non-Muslim authority that would produce a sort of anomy of identity, law, and morality in which there would no longer be a "true" form of Islam.

The Role of Jihadist Endeavor in the Definition of Being a Muslim

There is here a common element to the Jihadist visions embodied by *al-Qāʿida* and the Islamic State. The need to defend Islam behooves no longer just a part of the *umma (fard al-kifāya)* that is responsible for armed combat, but as many Muslims as possible, even all of them. It is therefore a question of an individual duty *(fard al- ʿayn)*, and all believers can grasp the necessity of joining the war effort through armed combat, financial donations, prayer, or intellectual struggle. This kind of approach largely explains why any Muslim is likely to join a Jihadist organization according to the theorists concerned. The radicalization of certain Muslims today echoes a process of enrollment more than a process of recruitment in that radicalization precedes the relationship to

---

[13] These debates form another part of the question of allegiance and disavowal *(al-walāʾ wa al-barāʾ)* in Islam, interpreted by the clergy in such a way as to produce both the religious conditions of obedience to a power and the conditions of its dispute (Wagemakers 2012a).

jihād. The space of conducting armed *jihād* thus now involves believers whose motivation relates to the desire to defend the *umma* under threat and the desire to take part in a violent project that implies permanent war. Taking part in armed *jihād* is at the crossroads of considerations that are no longer only of a religious motivation but also of a "de-secularized" reason for violent action. Indeed, the analysis of trajectories of radicalized individuals leads one to question the significance of religious socialization, and in so doing, the anchoring in an institutionalized Islamic imaginary. Even if radicalized individuals, including proclaimed leaders of contemporary armed *jihād*, refer to ambitions of embodying a vanguard *(al-ṭalī'a)* that is strong enough to put all principles of Islam into practice (starting with the "combat on the path of God" *(al-jihād fī sabīl li-lāh)*), one can wonder whether this space of Jihadism is not at the intersection of other motivational dynamics. These dynamics could include a pre-existing appetite for violence. In this respect, given the repetition of the same sociological profiles of radicalized individuals over the past several years (young, weak religious education, belonging to the most socio-economically disenfranchised groups, prior involvement in "classical" criminal circles), one wonders about the use of Jihadism as a grammar of dispute in broad terms. In this respect, religious intensification is the consequence of social and political radicalization.

On the other hand, contemporary Jihadism is differentiated from other historical forms of armed *jihād* by a radical reworking of the construction that has prevailed for several centuries. In terms of religious theorists (clerics), the figure of the enemy now takes on multiple forms and justifies in this respect a permanent state of war. This is because the lack of adhesion to the caliphate plan (in the case of the Islamic State) is equivalent to a declaration of war. Thus, there is potential or real martial action among the sole "true" believers who have understood that the Muslim faith involves not only a spiritual, cultural, and social ethics but also a state allegiance to an entity in constant search of expansion. Armed *jihād* is thus no longer directed against the outside or inside enemy but potentially against any co-religionist whose refusal to swear allegiance to the Islamic State Jihadist way is seen as an act of disloyalty against Islam. From this emerges a large gap between Jihadism as conceptualized by *al-Qāʿida* theorists and that imagined by the Islamic State, in that the former never considered Muslims who did not join the group as directly at fault, viewing them instead as a mass that needs to be convinced and mobilized through victories against the enemies of Islam. On the contrary, in the vision of the Islamic State, the field of adversity potentially reaches any person refusing to reinforce the Jihadist agenda. The main consequence of this is to divorce, morally, politically, and in terms of identity, the self-proclaimed vanguard from the rest of the believers, through a bond of both solidarity and disqualification. Indeed, since the responsibility of armed *jihād* is in this perspective supposed to be ensured by all Muslims, the fact that only one portion of the *umma* decides, in the case of Jihadism as theorized by the Islamic State, to gain lands of the Caliphate ends up dividing the mother country. The understanding of armed *jihād* as a collective responsibility results in separating Muslims almost ontologically between those who accept responsibility and the others who are disqualified for refusing to consider that the service of religion is accompanied by a military component. As such, the vanguard, put at the center of the reflection within Jihadism as conceived by *al-Qāʿida*, takes on a more radical definition, to the point of being confused in certain types of discourse as the one legitimate perimeter of the *umma*. The participation in armed *jihād* thus symbolizes, in the final analysis, the criteria of Islamic belonging. In this regard, this conception participates in a new definition of the Muslim identity since participation in the armed effort (such as it is understood by the Islamic State Organization) in reality determines affiliation to the religion. From this perspective, Jihadist commitment is no longer a violent engagement but an exclusive adherence to a religious community that is erecting itself in a relationship of exclusivity and exclusion with co-religionists who refuse to migrate toward Islamic State-ruled territories or fight in their country of origin in order to reinforce the permanent state of war. The category of "Muslim civilian" is thus disappearing, and no longer has relevance. Today, Jihadism (Islamic State-like more specifically) is interpreted as the victory of the continuous martial state, contrary to the exceptional nature that characterized it in past definitions of armed *jihād* (Khadduri 1955; Hashmi 2002; Crone 2004).

How to Strategize and Lead Jihadism Militarily?

The Jihadist mold has also raised new questions regarding ways of producing, spreading, and organizing waves of violence against people who are targeted in response to their supposed animosity toward and/or betrayal of Islam. Radicalization is thus observed not only in intellectual debates regarding the definition of categories of actors involved in armed *jihād*, but also in the appropriation of new forms of violence. It is a political act because it is part of a vision of war as a phenomenon that pits good against evil from a metaphysical point of view, while following a specific agenda that intends to change political structures (borders, sovereignty, etc.) and overthrow power relations (foreign influences, structures of alliances, international balance of powers, etc.). Radicalization must therefore be understood as part of a broader political struggle, where the local or national theater of operation obeys the same rationales of military and political antagonism that involve co-religionists in other regions of the world. The actor of Jihadism, living as a soldier of Islam, is seen as global and thus must act a global way. All means of waging war are allowed, as long as the theorists of Jihadism accept these methods. The lack of a Muslim army (here obviously Jihadist) in a non-Muslim society capable of leading the fight in the name of God makes underground action necessary. On the contrary, when the theater of operation involves an army understood in the classic sense of the term, radicalization is understood as an engagement in a group of fighters involved in one or several conflicts.

Joining a Foreign Jihadist Movement.

It is estimated that around 35,000 people were until recently in Jihadist organizations implanted in the Levant (Lister 2016). International Jihadists illustrate a dynamic of squad formation of modern armed *jihād*, whose implementation is at once disparate and international. *Al-Qāʿida*'s strategy was to take part in all conflicts in which Muslim populations were implicated in order to redirect the ideological meaning of their struggle toward a Jihadist vision (strategy of the "jihadization" of conflicts). However, the main armies were not made up of international fighters; this territorial and social paradigm shift initiated by *al-Qāʿida* experienced a radical change over the last few years with the emergence of the Caliphate plan. Here, squad formation means participating in the construction of a national religious army. The use of a military resource that straddles different continents represents one of the two faces of contemporary phenomena of radicalization. Becoming radicalized can resemble engagement in a military structure with a statist ambition just as much as it can be committing violence in one's country of origin. The former illustrates a change of scale compared to past phenomena of building an army under the authority of an identified Muslim power in the aim of re-establishing all or part of the *umma* in its rights. This is indeed a question of structuring not only a military movement whose action is no longer bounded in space and time but also of moving toward a meticulous destruction of the international order. Squad formation (referring to a globalized military vanguard) is thus part of a global geopolitical project that illustrates the specificity of modern Jihadism, namely that the only real way to defend Islam and Muslims is no longer in the search for an *ex ante* order but the toppling down of all current political forms that are portrayed as contradictory with the religious norm. The process of enrollment that characterizes this part of radicalization does not fit the mold of a temporary draft, but rather an almost definitive mass rising, since the aim is indeed geopolitical upheaval. The relationship to time is also radically different since the victory of the *umma* is seen as consubstantial to the destruction of any type of adversity. Being seen as hostile toward Islam only once can justify becoming a target. Since the conflict is now global, squad formation embodies the embryo of a transnational army. This aspect of radicalization thus evokes a form of normalization over time, since the formation of an enduring army brought to fight against an increasing number of enemies is the accepted purpose. This squad formation is radical in that it involves integration in an extremist movement, but the process in itself is classical since it is comparable to the formation of groups of fighters out of a transnational social basis. This once more reinforces the hypothesis of a specificity of modern Jihadism compared to the history of armed *jihād* of past centuries, to the extent that the globalization of recruitment is much more a case of globalization of contemporary forms of violence than the reproduction of a multi-secular religious imaginary.

Terrorist Radicalization

Another substantial development in the way the Jihadist offer is available in the strategic space is the legitimation and use of terrorism, even though the latter is not theorized as such by the clerics and activists concerned. The understanding of violence in modern Jihadism is thus part of a political conception since it serves specific strategic goals. The war that is waged against enemies as diverse as some Arab regimes or certain non-Muslim powers (Western or otherwise) is a matter of perpetuating politics and religion by other means. Ordaining, conceiving, and leading a martial situation, through which Jihadist groups aim to carry out a religious plan, consequently involve resolving the question of how to wage war, and in their case expanding its meaning to include the use of terrorism (the secular term interpreted in this vision as the continuation of the sacred war by other means). More specifically, thinking of themselves as those who initiate a response to violence committed against Islam and Muslims, the use of terrorism is justified because the impression that their enemies are waging a total war reinforces its legitimacy. Notably, in the Jihadist literature, suffering from civilian losses during conflicts and/or military interventions determines the targeting of other civilians in Jihadist violence. Major differences between the vision of *al-Qāʿida* and the Islamic State Organization in the engagement of non-military individuals include the impossibility of avoiding collateral victims, and the inclusion of civilians in the field of adversaries. In these two understandings of armed *jihād*, it is justified to carry out actions dedicated to spreading terror within primarily non-fighting populations.

As seen previously, the Islamic State has extended the field of injustice and alongside an expansionist strategy that changes the parameters of engagement of certain Muslims worldwide in modern Jihadism, terrorist radicalization has undergone important developments. The sociology of targets, as well as the modes of action used, has substantially transformed. From the *al-Qāʿida* generation to that of the Islamic State Organization, the goals have switched from institutional to cultural ones. While this does not mean that both groups are not interested in the other category, their two core targets are no less distinguished by a different ambition. In the first case, the use of terrorism, as illustrated by the targeting of the Pentagon, the White House, and the World Trade Center in September 2001, is explained by the desire to attack symbols of U.S. power and "arrogance." The United States is indeed a far-off enemy but present enough in Arab countries to influence a number of states against which Usāma b. Lāden was rebelling (Kepel and Milelli 2010). The shift in political orientation thus seems to be the main objective of the terrorist project. Even the attacks of March 11, 2004, against civilians in Madrid in the Atocha, El Pozo del Tio Raimundo, and Santa Eugenia train stations, arose from a violent reaction to Spain's participation in a military coalition in Iraq in the spring of 2003. The actions were undertaken with a view to punish a belligerent state and discourage any possible actor from invading a Muslim country. In a similar way, the killing of several members of the newspaper *Charlie Hebdo* was part of a specific rationale since the enemy, represented by artists and journalists making fun of the prophet of Islam, was sentenced to death. This certainly aimed to send a message of terror, but also to react to what is interpreted as a bilateral provocation (*Charlie Hebdo* seen as outraging Muslims for example). Moreover, the method of organization of such attacks is characterized by the involvement of an organization responsible for, at the very least, targeting legitimate enemies, but also of financing and even almost entirely preparing the terrorist attack in question (Hoffman and Reinares 2014). This sponsor's paradigm is the trademark of the *al-Qāʿida* generation.

On the other hand, today terrorism seems to be part of a viral paradigm. Traditionally, Jihadist terrorism (similarly to nearly any other type of terrorism prior to it) was characterized by a classical relationship that unites three parties. In this three-parties scheme, two of which are linked by both a common ideological and organizational affiliation in the aim of damaging a third category of people (two against one). However, this situation seems to be increasingly replaced with a new one that I call "viral terrorism." I use the term "viral" to the extent that, aside from the attacks of November 13, 2015, in Paris and those of March 22, 2016, in Brussels, there exists now a phenomenon of diffuse cultural influence. Indeed, a sort of moral preparation precedes acting. New generations of Jihadists using terrorist methods adopt a *modus operandi* through which the act is committed, and the figure of the enemy is specified. Armed combat is a form of acculturation before being the fruit of violent action. The shift to violence functions in a viral model in that a relation of hostility is introduced or reinforced among certain people who will implement it with violence that they themselves design. Indeed, there is a substantial amount of individual creativity, given that the ideological aspects are known (permanent state of war, identification of the enemy, etc.) while the practical details of the terrorist act are left up to the perpetrator. It is thus not so much a question of an act that is ordered as it is of terrorist careers being triggered. Hostility toward others is implemented using Jihadist methods even though it could have been undertaken using symbolic, verbal, or (more classically) physical violence. Terrorist radicalization seems here to be joining the Jihadist agenda as used by the Islamic State but is determined and based on motivations that are more complex. Historical armed *jihād* operates according to a clear and circumstantial definition of the enemy and of the action to be set in motion. Yet, since contemporary Jihadism is a systemization of martial law, it leads, primarily in its most current form, to a dilution of the relationship to *jihād*. Any hostile phenomenon (even a non-religious one) thus finds itself being included in an imaginary that was structured in another region of the world. The Islamic State offers the conditions for converting existing social or interpersonal tensions into a sacred battle. In this respect, the opportunities for armed *jihād* are even more substantial since they are atomized and part of an individual biography. The trajectory of a Muslim can push them to convert frustrations and unease into a Jihadist imaginary, leading them to consider their environment through a radical religious prism. The homology between personal psychological tensions and the desire to defend co-religionists in other regions of the world substantially explains terrorist radicalization. As they are steeped in a transnational ideological combat, local interactions involving certain Muslims become "jihadized." The suicidal drive, the desire to hurt a despised group, or even the feeling of solidarity with co-religionists pushes the Jihadist imaginary to be considered from a certain degree of opportunism. Thus, the ideological supply does not necessarily generate the demand. Instead, certain social profiles seize an opportunity to express in religious words their pre-existing radicalism by identifying a doctrinal system provided by the Islamic State. The current Jihadist generation thus no longer only functions based on the jihadization of a tangible conflict in a given world region. Instead, it functions on a jihadization of social relations and tensions within a given society, which is often not even predominately Muslim (Neumann **2016**; Rabasa and Benard **2014**).

The sponsor's paradigm has not necessarily been abandoned as it seems to be privileged when the Islamic State wishes to intervene in the phase of military withdrawal in the Middle East for instance. However, the simultaneous emergence of a viral model in which the relationship seems inversed (mental radicalization preceding violent engagement) undeniably reinforces the psychological effect of these new forms of terrorism. This leads us to question whether it is possible to speak of a revolution of the Islamic State since despite a probable end as an aspiring state, its imaginary will still be able to influence or even spark a number of individual missions. In this sense, the terrorist radicalization that has emerged in the past few years illustrates a form of revolution since it is based on a new grammar. Jihadism has become a mass counterculture. This is marked by a strong combination of seeking to cause terror with individualization. It then needs to pervade, for a number of years to come, the imaginary of actors whose personal profiles and motivations are as diversified as ever. In this sense, it seems justified to evoke a new generation of Jihadism that embodies a real break with what we have seen up until now.

References

Abou El Fadl, K. 1999. The Rules of Killing at War: An Inquiry into Classical Sources. *The Muslim World* 89 (2): 155–157.
Abou El Fadl, K. 2001. *Rebellion and Violence in Islamic Law*. Cambridge: Cambridge University Press.
Al-Rasheed, M. 2010. *A History of Saudi Arabia*. Cambridge: Cambridge University Press.
Bonney, R. 2004. *Jihad: From Qur'an to Bin Laden*. Basingstoke: Palgrave Macmillan.
Calvert, J. 2010. *Sayyid Qutb and the Origins of Radical Islamism*. New York, NY: Columbia University Press.
Cavatorta, F., and F. Merone, eds. 2017. *Salafism after the Arab Awakening: Contending with People's Power*. New York, NY: Oxford University Press.
Cook, D. 2005. *Understanding Jihad*. Berkeley, CA: University of California Press.
Crone, P. 2004. *God's Rule-Government and Islam: Six Centuries of Medieval Islamic Thought*. New York, NY: Columbia University Press.
Gerges, F.A. 2009. *The Far Enemy: Why Jihad Went Global*. Cambridge: Cambridge University Press.
Gerges, F.A. 2011. *The Rise and Fall of Al-Qaeda*. Oxford: Oxford University Press.
Gerges, F.A. 2017. *ISIS: A History*. Princeton, NJ: Princeton University Press.
Hashim, A.S. 2017. *The Caliphate at War: The Ideological, Organizational and Military Innovations of Islamic State*. Oxford: Oxford University Press.
Hashmi, S.S., ed. 2002. *Islamic Political Ethics: Civil Society, Pluralism, and Conflict*. Princeton, NJ: Princeton University Press.
Hatina, M. 2012. Redeeming Sunni Islam: Al-Qaida's Polemic Against the Muslim Brothers. *British Journal of Middle East Studies* 39 (1): 101–113.
Hoffman, B., and F. Reinares, eds. 2014. *The Evolution of the Global Terrorist Threat: From 9/11 to Osama Bin Laden's Death*. New York, NY: Columbia University Press.
Holbrook, D. 2014. *The Al-Qaeda Doctrine: The Framing and Evolution of the Leadership's Public Discourse*. London: Bloomsbury Academic.
Kepel, G. 2003a. *Muslim Extremism in Egypt: The Prophet and Pharaoh*. Berkeley, CA: University of California Press.
Kepel, G. 2003b. *Jihad: The Trail of Political Islam*. Cambridge, MA: Harvard University Press.
Kepel, G., and J.-P. Milelli, eds. 2010. *Al Qaeda in Its Own Words*. Cambridge, MA: Harvard University Press.
Khadduri, M. 1955. *War and Peace in the Law of Islam*. Baltimore, MD: Johns Hopkins University Press.

Lia, B. 1999. *The Society of the Muslim Brothers in Egypt: The Rise of an Islamic Mass Movement*. Reading: Ithaca Press.

Lister, C. 2016. *The Syrian Jihad: Al-Qaeda, the Islamic State and the Evolution of an Insurgency*. New York, NY: Oxford University Press.

Manne, R. 2017. *The Mind of the Islamic State: ISIS and the Ideology of the Caliphate*. Amherst: Prometheus Books.

Martinez, L. 2000. *The Algerian Civil War: 1990–1998*. New York, NY: Columbia University Press.

Meijer, R., ed. 2009. *Global Salafism: Islam's New Religious Movement*. New York, NY: Oxford University Press.

Neumann, P.R. 2016. *Radicalized: New Jihadists and the Threat to the West*. London: I.B. Tauris.

Peters, R. 1996. *Jihad in Classical and Modern Islam: A Reader*. Princeton, NJ: Markus Wiener Publishers.

Rabasa, A., and C. Benard. 2014. *Eurojihad: Patterns of Islamist Radicalization and Terrorism in Europe*. Cambridge: Cambridge University Press.

Roy, O. 2017. *Jihad and Death: The Global Appeal of the Islamic State*. New York, NY: Oxford University Press.

Schmitt, C. 2007. *The Concept of the Political*. Chicago, MI: University of Chicago Press.

Staffel, S., and A. Awan, eds. 2016. *Jihadism Transformed: Al-Qaeda and Islamic State's Global Battle of Ideas*. Oxford: Oxford University Press.

Turner, J.A. 2014. *Religious Ideology and the Roots of the Global Jihad*. Basingstoke: Palgrave Macmillan.

Wagemakers, J. 2012a. The Enduring Legacy of the Second Saudi State: Quietist and Radical Wahhabi Contestations of *Al-Wala' wal-Bara'*. *International Journal of Middle East Studies* 44 (1): 93–110.

Wagemakers, J. 2012b. *A Quietist Jihadi: The Ideology and Influence of Abu Muhammad Al-Maqdisi*. Cambridge: Cambridge University Press.

Wasserstein, D.J. 2017. *Black Banners of ISIS: The Roots of the New Caliphate*. New Haven, CT: Yale University Press.

CHAPTER 9

Salafism in Context: Understanding the Issue of Ideological and Social Permeability, and the Value Placed on Quietism, Political Participation and Violence

Abstract This section focuses on the question of the links between Salafism and jihadism today, and more specifically on the way in which these two currents are increasingly opposed to each other, and even give rise to major ideological, sociological, and political reconfigurations.

Keywords Jihad/Jihadism · Al-Qaeda/Islamic state organization · Islamism · Muslim brotherhood · Terrorism · Violence · Orthodoxy · Orthopraxy

If there is a question that marks today debate related to Salafism, it is certainly that of doctrinal and social divergences that have emerged during the previous decades as to the "orthodox" relationship to be maintained with political powers. This today produces a crucial fault line for understanding the evolutions of contemporary Islamic fundamentalism and their impact on the current global political reformations, starting with certain conflicts whose scope more than ever stretches worldwide. Salafism, Wahhabism, Jihadism, and Islamism: these notions often lead to confusion in that they insist, as indicated by their names, on a profound phenomenon of ideologization of religion, even though rigorously analyzing them shows not only very different histories but also an often-strong relationship of competition, even of disqualification between these faces of contemporary Muslim fundamentalism competing for the hegemony over the incarnation of "true" Islam. The issue is even more complicated in that rivalries (nonetheless undeniable) can also be coupled with doctrinal, sociological, and political permeability which are also observed, and which explain a number of current debates, beginning with that related to the "radicalization" of certain actors and their violent strategies.

Salafism and Violence: Is Political Change Desirable? if Yes, How to Achieve It?

If Salafist reformism is both the means and the end as we have seen, is violence a part of the possible paths for returning to the early times? The question seems to be even legitimate given the habit of splitting Salafism into different branches today seems to have been done, starting with academics, in the aim of proposing a more detailed contemporary reading of this phenomena. Thus, being Salafist is supposed to refer to an unequal disposition within the Islamic field, being orthodox thus granting a status of "virtuoso" of faith in the sense of Max Weber which evokes "an unequal religious qualification of men" by virtue of which is split a mass religion and an elitist belief founded on the possession of a "necessary charisma for guaranteeing the permanent certitude of grace" (Weber 1993). In this sense, although the preaching movement aiming at the adhesion of the greatest number, a logic of exclusive salvation characterizes certain Salafists in the name of the belief of being the best able (or the only ones able) to follow "the right path". Reviving the faith of the Ancients gives the feeling of a religious excellency that is nonetheless differentiated (sometimes radically) when the question of the relationship to the other is raised. Indeed, how should the heterodoxy of the social realm resulting from religious heterodoxy be managed?

From this emerges a utilitarian reasoning in the name of which the cleric in charge of the task of bringing the *umma* back on "the right path" must weigh the pros and cons when considering the authorization or prohibitions of certain means of preaching and reforming society. Spreading the "true" belief is a necessity as the salvation of humanity depends on it, whose nature *(al-fiṭra)* is to reply to the call of the

Creator. Nonetheless, the same *ʿulamā* recognize multiple realities while acknowledging the obligation of constantly combining faith and practice. In itself, this effort of disclosing the truth is the equivalent of *jihād*, whose understanding did split contemporary Salafist branches and leads to opposing by virtue (among other considerations) of the right relationship to have toward the question of political change. Defending the plan of the return to the roots is here a case of *jihād* since it corresponds to the re-establishment of a "more Islamic" situation than what contemporary reality allows us to observe.

Today, Salafism can then be seen as a specter of religious combinations between these three practical questions: who should take the responsibility of preaching, including at the political level in order to meet the challenges faced by the *umma*? Against which dangers should one react both on a strictly religious level as well as socially and politically? What means should be used and within which kinds of constraints? It thus appears that there are currently several faces of Salafism that need to be studied. The Salafism of the Saudi State has historically promoted a strong social conservatism while creating spaces of intervention worldwide in order to spread Islam but also in order to come to the aid of Muslims threatened because of certain conflicts. Sharing this desire to help their co-religionists and to reform contemporary morals, quietist Salafists envision their preaching as occurring in the social and cultural sphere but not at an institutional or political level. If their majority sees Saudi action in good light, their positioning is based on the idea that the renouncing of political activism is a good thing, as the latter generates more sedition than stability in the end. Clerics and chiefs of certain Muslim nations, by taking charge of the defense of the *umma*, confer the rest of their co-religionists called upon to prove their obedience against the protection they benefit from. A political ethics, despite the refusal of certain Salafists to call it that, societal change is left to the discretion of the cleric-prince duopoly.

Other imitators, saying they are aware that such a way of thinking leads to aporia due to the need of reforming the State without which the social body cannot find the conditions of a more Islamic life, developed a participationnist ethics and represent today a new generation of political Islam,[1] historically embodied by movements following in the wake

---

[1] The "Party of Light" *(ḥizb al-nūr)* that was founded in 2011 during the revolutionary dynamics in Egypt is an example of this type of Salafism nowadays.

of the Muslim Brotherhood[2] (founded in 1927). Legitimizing the existence of and participation in elections in order to compete for power, this face of Salafism involves the modern categories of politics (democracy, constitution, elections, parliament, etc.) in the aim of orienting them toward greater conformity with religious norms. In their eyes, power sees itself as a potentially vacant place, which authorizes those who revolt against the prince, turning against an authority wanted by God,[3] to claim it—unlike quietists for whom it is at some point a sacred space. As for quietist Salafists living in a non-Muslim majority context, in order to escape symbolic domination as well as the risk of perdition which characterizes the path taken by society that is blind to religious principles, the migration of salvation *(al-hijra)*, like the first Muslim communities having fled *Mekka* for *Madīna*, is a way out. A journey that is both moral and physical toward Islamic land, this illustrates again that Salafism is the Islam of globalization. Another face is that of groups taking part in a cultural and ideological competition with their environment and which attempt by social activism or low intensity violent strategies to assert their radicalism. This is the case of certain entities such as the *Riders of Pride (fursān al-ʿizza)* in France, *Sharia4UK*, *Sharia4Belgium*, and other Salafist student groups from *Al-Mannūba* University in Tunis.

Finally, according to Salafists that claim to also be Jihadist, the idea of a power (even held by Muslims) that is not subject to criticism, or even overthrowing, symbolizes an abomination. The need to assure the stability of the social body cannot replace the need for moral reform of leaders, whether clerics or princes. Thus, any decision taken by a government claiming Islam must be studied in-depth by the same *sharīʿa* that applies to the people, and if it is proved that the latter is wrong, it enters the realm of frontal reform even if certain clerics are opposed to it. *Jihād* is not only here the call to reason and morality but also a "combat through the sword" to re-establish the rights of the dogma. Widening the space of authenticity must first be done against regimes which, as long as they are not replaced, will prevent the return to the roots. As for non-Muslim states, a contractual relationship links these Jihadist Salafists to the latter, which anticipates relationships based on a certain number of

---

[2] *Jamāʿat al-ikhwān al-muslimīn*.

[3] The means of social change coming from the fact that the cleric, because of his good advice, is supposed to have the ear of the prince and thus the possibility of transforming politics.

classical interests managed by a form of customary laws (related to business, economics, diplomacy, etc.) but which can be considered the realm of martial law if the *umma* is targeted, just like the reasoning of the *al-Qāʿida* generation against the Soviet Union, the United States as well as any other countries accused of attacking Muslims. For instance, being accused of causing the oppression of Palestinians and the theft of their land means (among other criticisms) the right to war in the perspective of Usāma b. Lāden, who justified the September 11 attacks as the fruit of the need to export the conflict "against Islam" on the land of a belligerent country and the possibility of targeting civilians, the enemy acting similarly against co-religionists. A martial construction of religion and politics by virtue of which forms of violence (normally prohibited) are authorized, including against oneself as illustrated by the suicide attacks (committing suicide being theoretically considered a sin because it is a negation of the divine decree), the main motivation of Jihadism in the twentieth century is the desire to ideologically and militarily rearm the *umma* against its aggressors, and this narrative largely explains its success, in addition in a context of a state that is bankrupt and in conflict with its civilians.

Beyond the Fragmentation of Salafism: Is Jihadism Getting Autonomized?

There is thus an ideological permeability between different conceptions of Salafism that are hard to refute. Needed to defend divine unicity, religious identity seen as faith and practice or the need to accept what pleases God and to renounce what is condemned by Him are cross-cutting themes. Nonetheless, Salafism cannot be confounded with a specific branch in that it is first of all a dynamic movement characterized by its topographical relationship to history. Echoing in reality multiple and sometimes opposing ways to think about religious content, this reformism is first a matrix with which a debate is organized from which various intellectual and political ethics can emerge. If Salafism has historically produced Jihadism (without forgetting that certain evolutions related to Islamic branches resulting from the Muslim Brotherhood also played an important role), it has also led to modernizing visions as illustrated by the enlightened Salafism *(al-salafiyya al-tanwīriyya)*[4] among some clerics in the nineteenth century who wanted to take all of the benefits of progress which did not contradict with their view of Islamic principles. In this respect, it is both true and false to say that Salafism is the ideological infrastructure of phenomena of political violence observable in several regions of the contemporary world, and which takes the form both of terrorism (based on a sponsor connected with an established organization in the Middle East that wants to strike a country at a given time, or that is viral, meaning by virtue of a dynamic of acculturation in the name of which an individual is not a member of a movement but manifests their personal animosities according to a Jihadist grammar) and the adhesion in a fighting army within a theater of specific operations. If there is a historicity of Jihadist movement that is today known, this shows that the role of Saudi Arabia and the religious legitimation that benefited groups taking part in conflicts involving Muslims starting in the 1980s, but also that Salafist as a religious practice does not generally create the conditions for a particular attraction to Jihadism. In order words, on a micro-sociological level, the reasons for radicalism should first be sought elsewhere than in religious socialization, whereas at the macropolitical level the emergence of Jihadism is explained in part by the birth of a Salafist paradigm during the twentieth century. In this respect, it is possible to emphasize the existence of a phenomena of autonomization of Jihadism today in that the social trajectories leading to this violent ideology do not necessarily meet those of puritan careers, whether in Muslim or non-Muslim majority countries. It is as though Jihadism became during our time a school in and of itself, certainly sharing a common heritage with other forms of Salafism, but whose legitimation of military combat for Islam (moreover a total form as can be observed with the Islamic State Organization) and the ambition to upset the world political arena against the backdrop of offensive millenarism and precipitated eschatologism makes a hybrid movement more than a reformist force over the long term.

Three ideas must hereby be highlighted. First, the purely doctrinal dimension of the connections between Salafist revivalism and violent Jihadism. From a macro point of view, Jihadism espouses a form of religious morphology that stems from a Salafist approach. Both conceptually

---

[4] Embodied by key Muslim figures such as Jamāl al-Dīn al-Afghānī (1838–1897) and Muḥammad ʿAbduh (1849–1905).

and discursively, these two manifestations of present-day Muslim fundamentalism seem to share a very similar epistemology whose grammar was historically developed as a response to a common matrix. Does this commonality reveal an absolute identity between the two or rather does the latter proceed from the former? Second, one should question a possible homology between the two. The sociological trajectories of Jihadist fighters are often different from those of many Salafists. Besides, Salafist adepts have developed dissimilar political considerations. We observe an increasingly clear and explicit tendency where different sides of Islamic fundamentalism disqualify each other. A differentiation or even proliferation is observable in the Salafist field due to some factors that need clarifying. This leads Jihadism to be perceived as a distinct school increasingly diverging from the Salafist fundamentalism. The third idea is a sociological point of view. The geographical context and human resources of the Jihadists who support religiously motivated violence differ from those of most Salafists who are likewise religiously fundamentalist but politically opposed to violence. Moreover, we see an ideologization of Islam whose content substantially differs from that of the most common type of Salafist preaching. A closer examination of Jihadist phenomenon shows that socio-cultural isolation and alienation facilitates adoption of Jihadist views, and that Jihadists have different social profiles. The religious justification of violence as, for instance, represented by the Islamic State Organization shows also differences among other fundamentalists. This leads to the conclusion that the Jihadist socialization process would be now largely detached from any prior fundamentalist processes and a new "Jihadist ethics" might be under construction.

Salafism and Jihadism: A Common Doctrinal Heritage

Salafism is a long-standing movement within the Islamic tradition; yet it is not fair to think of it as a totally coherent school of thought. It today comprises diverse groups. The common assumption of the Salafist belief is that Muslims have deviated in time from the "original" Islam and thereby ended up with various groups that have differently and aberrantly interpreted the normative sources of Islam. Contemporary scholarship on Salafism tends to classify the Salafist narrative into three main groups

(Wiktorowicz 2006). First group are those Salafists who preach a particular position on political activism. They seek to serve their revivalist goals through classical political activism designed to bring a party to power wishing to reform the society in question in the direction of a greater "authenticity." The second group are those who give legitimacy to Muslim regimes and tend to suppress all other forms of political opposition contesting these regimes. They justify their position by arguing that any sedition *(al-fitna)*, which is not forestalled, might endanger the socio-political order without which the religious orthodoxy could be threatened. The followers of the third group, on the contrary, justify use of violence and incite the armed struggle aimed at overthrowing any enemy who, whether "nominally" Muslim or not, opposes the restoration of the "primordial" and "authentic" model. These diverse, even antagonistic, Salafist positions within the same matrix can be explained by the different politico-religious constructions that stem from divergent understandings of the preaching of the leading Salafist *'ulamā* and their fundamental concepts.

Historically speaking, Salafism has evolved as a response to several crises that were responded by a number of influential scholars/clerics whose puritanical reform attempts in turn set the keystones of Salafist epistemology. In these scholars' views, these crises paved way to certain deviant beliefs and practices and in some cases, they even put people out of Islam. Their puritanical reforms or counter-reforms hence targeted to revive "genuine" Islam and restore the norm again with reference to the Ancients.

In traditional Salafist literature, genuine *tawḥīd* ("unicity" or "oneness") requires asserting three types: (i.) *tawḥīd al-ulūhiyya*, or the Oneness of God's Divinity; that is He is alone worthy to be worshiped as God; (ii.) *tawḥid al-rubūbiyya*, or the Oneness of God's Lordship; that is it is only God Himself who is capable of performing certain acts such as creating, bestowing life and sustenance, bringing life and death,[5] etc.; (iii.) *tawḥīd al-asmā' wa-l-ṣifāt*, oneness of God's Names and Attributes,

---

[5] This is why, as we have seen above, suicide is theoretically an abomination because it is God who creates life and takes it back when the time comes. A person choosing to die by suicide therefore contradicts the divine sovereignty that alone generates life and death, whereas Jihadist thought values the martyr *(shāhid)* who makes the conscious choice to die for the good of the umma. This valorization can only be understood because Jihadism is built on a martial vision of Islam according to which what is normally prohibited becomes permitted or even desirable in the event of a conflict requiring defense against enemies.

that is, God's description of Himself (first of all in the *Qur'ān*) implies an ontological specificity. He is the only One who perfectly claims for Greatness, Perfection, Power, or Knowledge. Although these categories exist in humans, they cannot be compared to what these terms cover when God speaks of Himself. There is a consensus among the Salafist groups on this tripartite understanding of *tawḥīd*. This consensus is also shared more generally within Sunnism. Jihadists, however, have been adding a fourth element, namely *tawḥīd al-ḥākimiyya*, or Oneness of God' Sovereignty. According to this latter Jihadist extra, a society can be managed only by the strict respect of religious injunctions commanded by God Himself. More precisely, this conception is based on the idea that the structures of a society (political, legal, identity, cultural, etc.) must never be in conflict with the divine commands. For example, according to this view, the Salafist reform cannot be limited merely to power in a given society. All that would be seen as a failure to unite Muslims and to defend themselves could legitimize the act of "turning against those in authority." Moreover, *sharīʿa* represents one of the preferred means of serving *tawḥīd* on earth and is always superior to any regime, however nominally Muslim it may be. Because, the sincerity of a Muslim believer, they argue, requires, first and foremost, allegiance to Islam as an integralist, "uncompromising" and "radical" faith and practice. As an extension of this argument, the Jihadists claim that a "violation" of *sharīʿa* authorizes physical and armed *jihād* and sanctions an uprising against a "failing" authority.

Jihadist Differentiation from Salafism

Various forms of conflict that take place within militant Jihadism make it possible to seriously question, or at least qualify, the thesis that there is a structured continuity between fundamentalist socialization of Salafism and violent commitment of Jihadism. *Al-Qāʿida* and the Islamic State are certainly the two major representatives of the phenomena of espousal of the Jihadist conceptual imagination. Their respective interpretations of *jihād*, however, sheds light on how today's Jihadism has begun to differ from Salafism. The case of *al-Qāʿida* exemplifies the re-organization of Salafism as a Jihadist ideology. The Afghanistan War in the 1980s, which took place against the backdrop of the final days of the Cold War, set the context for this re-organization. Here, we saw for the first time in the history of Islam a discussion on initiating a world revolution with the ultimate aim of bringing a unique and exclusive sovereignty commanding the whole of the *umma*. Although the defense of fellow believers remained a central concern in the Afghan conflict, the later emergence of *al-Qāʿida* triggered a new form of global Jihadist insurgency that no longer claims to involve the *umma* within a particular geographical area only. In other words, *jihād* in this case ceased to be a form of violence that is limited to the duration of a particular war. This new form makes the claim of common identity between Salafism and Jihadism more questionable. While its will to unite the Islamic *umma* may be understood as an illustration of reviving an original norm (e.g., a return to the times of the "well-guided Caliphs" during the time of the *salaf*), an armed *jihād* has never been such disconnected from a specific time and place over the past centuries of Islamic history. This unbounded and perpetual nature is what constitutes the present-day novelty. On the other hand, even though the Islamic State Jihadists, unlike *al-Qāʿida*, have sought to establish the Caliphate in a particular territory, their case exemplifies not a Jihadist re-organization of Salafism but another kind of differentiation from it. The case of the Islamic State Organization indeed highlights two new phenomena: the growing sociological discontinuity between Salafism and Jihadism, and the emergence of a new type of Jihadist intent which is primarily motivated by total violence, and which relegates concerns about religious orthodoxy to the second place to be replaced, instead, by an apocalyptic discourse that transforms the conventional Salafist focus on redressing this world.

Empowerment of Jihadism: Violence Without Religious Socialization

From a macro sociological point of view, the emergence of Jihadism is often rightly explained by the emergence of a Salafist paradigm during the course of the twentieth century. On the micro-sociological level, however, the causes of the current phenomena of radicalization increasingly represent a clear disconnection between Salafist socialization and embracing use of violence. As the Saudi experience shows, religious (Islamic) framing of contemporary violence has been observed for a period of several years and in various countries. Yet, this was before violence was embraced as a consistent trajectory. Current Jihadism distinguishes itself by a dynamic of empowerment of people whose itineraries leading to this ideology fail to follow those of puritanical careers, both in majority and minority Muslim contexts. The Jihadist ideology, as we mostly observe in IS today, is today progressively becoming a different school itself. Although it shares a common heritage with other forms of Salafism, it legitimizes military struggle for Islam and aims to disrupt world politics in order to make itself a hybrid movement rather than an enduring force for Salafist reform. We still lack comparative, cross-sectional studies examining the number of people who had previously been part of a Salafist community and subsequently espoused the Jihadist conceptual imagination. Some research (Roy 2017; Khosrokhavar 2021), nevertheless suggest that in the majority of cases, the profiles of combatants from Europe or predominantly Muslim societies who joined *al-Qāʿida*, the Islamic State Organization or claimed to act out of ideological affiliation with them are marked by an absence of an ordered fundamentalist socialization that is observed within Salafist communities. This does not mean that the Salafist discourse does not generate or consolidate religious radicalism as we see a differentiation between Salafists and Jihadists. It rather indicates that the social disruption that today fuels support for Jihadism seems to be of another sort. Predisposition to embrace the legitimacy of the Islamic State's strategy of total violence often stems from an appetite for physical violence and the apocalyptic utopia which in fact spring from a secular rather than a religious form of socialization rather than any Salafist rooting that Jihadists claimed at the outset.

Besides observing this "Salafism-free Jihadism" in the life-path of most of the militants, present-day followers also demonstrate emergence of a new ethics of violence that proceeds mainly from individual initiatives. This individuality is not only about individual ideological affiliation independently from a Jihadist organization, but also is about individual the philosophy of violent action and its *modus operandi*. We see here a viral paradigm that illustrates the fact that Salafism and Jihadism have now become mutually distinct realities although the latter is empowered by the former. Nevertheless, Islamic State's theoreticians now trigger an independent Jihadist form which is characterized by and an essentially individual approach whereby identification, assimilation, and implementation of the call to violence take place at the individual, instead of a collective, level. In short, a considerable number this new Jihadist generation define themselves in terms of viral Jihadism. Armed combat here is a form of acculturation rather than the result of a military commitment. The transition to violence works in a viral mode where a hostility is first created or reinforced in certain individuals who then find reasons to nurture it as part of a relationship of violence which they will often themselves go on to decide just how it is translated into acts. There is, indeed, a large share of personal creativity in this. While the ideological contours are already given (i.e., a state of permanent war, the designation of the enemy, etc.), the practical aspects of the terrorist act are usually left up to the perpetrator himself to work out. We see here not so much of a sponsored action but rather the instigation of terrorist careers. Hostility to others is displayed in the form of *jihād* whereas it might have been expressed in the (more classical) form of symbolic, verbal, or physical violence. Terrorist radicalization then appears to espouse the Jihadist agenda as it is put forward by the Islamic State Organization; but it is actually driven by more complex mechanisms. Jihadism, essentially in its most recent form, leads to a dilution of the relationship with *jihād* as for instance highlighted in the previous chapter.

Apocalypticism of Islamic State Jihadism

Al-Qāʿida, the father-movement of global contemporary Jihadism, primarily aimed to fight against "the enemies of Islam" and to proliferate the centers of conflict without any territorialization strategy. Founded and headed by elders from *al-Qāʿida* (as well as form the Iraqi *baʿthī* regime), the Islamic State Organization (Gerges 2017), rather, breaks with this agenda to replace it with a revival of the Apocalypse. While apocalypticism is not absent from the literature ascribed to the Jihadist theoreticians of previous generations (Filiu 2012), the Islamic State design distinguishes itself by a specificity which largely accounts for its current success and which above all prevents it from being identified as a classical Salafist movement.

Its perception of future echoes the belief that it is now time to precipitate the end of the mundane times so as to hasten the final Day of Judgement *(yawm al-dīn)*. As such, the Islamic State Organization explicitly sees itself as an essential agent of "the end of time" whose members (leaders, clerics, inhabitants, soldiers, etc.) form a community of those "rescued" people. It is the only one who is able to correctly interpret the present time and "the signs of the hour" *(ʿalāmāt al-sāʿa)* which herald the demise of the terrestrial world and the imminence of final judgment. Hence, the idea of establishing and expanding an "Islamic State" reflects the desire both to defeat the enemies of Islam and to prepare the *umma* to achieve its salvation. The newly restored "Caliphate" on the rubble of "falsely" Islamic regimes is considered as being one of the most important signs heralding the coming of the (ultimate) hour. Establishing a political and religious structure claiming to be the ultimate one in history thus fulfills both an ideological purpose (ensuring Islam's triumph) and a soteriological one (ensuring the salvation of Muslims, for whom there is no longer any other horizon than that of the restored Caliphate). This is what makes the Islamic State experience such a specific movement as being the first that follows an eschatological logic in realizing its ultimate aim. As its teleological belief states that human history is inevitably leading to the Day of Judgement, the Islamic State people hold that the future is already heralded by the warning signs. Accordingly, the future of humanity will witness the ultimate collision of the forces of "good" and "evil," a logic of self-fulfilling prophecy. In their eyes, any event involving the Islamic State community should necessarily be interpreted in eschatological terms. At the root of Islamic State's militant activities (military, political, religious, etc.) runs this fundamental apocalyptic logic. The advent of the end of time, thus, must be saluted by membership to the organization.

Therefore, the phenomena of Jihadist commitment that have been unfolding before our eyes over recent years, whether they take the form of leaving for a warzone like Syria to fight or committing terrorist violence in a peaceful society, Western or not, seem to bypass the traditional Salafist conceptual imagination. The offensive apocalypticism and the idea of imminent end of the world had never been part of Salafist preaching before. The ideological distinction with classical Salafism reaches a climax here. In Salafism, the relationship to time and history includes no notion of any possible appropriation by the believers themselves. The "end" will come, but without any deliberate venture to restore the Caliphate through encouraging the "true" believers to actively join to the apocalyptic end. The ultimate purpose of Salafism has been rather purification and education *(al-taṣfiyya wal-tarbiyya)* within a framework of worldly puritanism. In other words, Muslims are not called upon to bring to an end by the Salafists because they continue to share the same time frame with those who are not Salafists. The Jihadism embodied by the Islamic State, on the other hand, is undeniably built upon a radically different conception of time and the believer's relationship to it.

Post-Islamic State Jihadism

Although it is difficult for the moment to confidently forecast the future of the Islamic State's Jihadist activities, one can still point to a certain number of potentially important changes to be expected over the coming years.

Considering its recent territorial demise, the Islamic State Organization must today deal with three issues in particular. Firstly, how can it recover from the forced eviction from, and the disappearance of, the proto state that the movement sought to build and extend? This represents the very foundation of its politico-military strategy and its conceptual imagination. Secondly, if offensive Islamic apocalypticism meant a fundamental rupture with the *al-Qāʿida* generation and made the Islamic State's hallmark, what will it do now with such a utopia whose one of founding and constitutive prophecies has already aborted? That is to say, what future is there for the Jihadists' apocalyptic illusion in the face of "unmet prophecies" (Bunzel 2017). Finally, rather than embodying the Salafist puritanical agenda, the Islamic State generation has emerged with embodying total violence that was conditioned by the Middle Eastern geopolitics. Should we expect the definite emergence of Jihadism as an independent current different than Salafism that opts for an all-out belligerent ethic with primary focus on violence and as such no more adheres to the latter's claim to embody the lasting Islam in everyday life? In other words, should we expect a schismatic event to occur in the Salafist matrix we have been studying?

An answer to these three questions could be that the Islamic State experience represents a truly radical transformation of Salafism. On the one hand, it shares certain principles of contemporary Salafism (such as the need to disavow what Islam is supposed to oppose). On the other hand, its apocalyptic strategy and intransigent emphasis on armed *jihād*, which are only a small part of the Salafist doctrinal heritage, make it quite unique. In other words, through hyper specialization in a discourse of violence and total belligerence, the Islamic State distances itself from modern Salafist revivalism that pursued to set up a symbolic authority focused on extolling the early days of Islam to address the anomic crises that different Muslim groups have gone through over the past few centuries. The Islamic State Organization certainly provides protection and meaning (under limited conditions) to social groups that demand violence, for instance, to some *sunnī* populations in the Levant, to the Western youth in rebellion or to the radicalized political players in the Arab world. However, it does not propose a lasting and genuinely structured narrative unlike, for example, that of the non-violent quietist Salafists. The latter's narrative can be more in tune with the codes and norms of the certainties of modernity, such as looking for material wealth while staying away from political activism (Adraoui 2020), moral radicalism for a social and cultural change without resorting to violence, opposition to grand ideologies that advocate transforming the world through violence. The post-IS Jihadism seems to be definitely less Salafist.

The above analysis indicates that while Salafism has taken a form of ideologization of Islam, Jihadism has further taken an ideologization of Salafism. Doctrinally and historically, both maintain a cognitive or political radicalization which generates a clear dichotomy between "true" believers and "deviant" others. Notwithstanding, it would be misleading to hastily conclude that at the present time, Salafism is the ideological infrastructure of Jihadism. Such a generalization holds a linear vision which assumes that wherever the former is adopted the latter necessarily emerges. It presumes a direct link between Salafism, violence, and Jihadism, or between ideology and ideologization. Salafism is believed to set the scene for the social and moral disruption which later prepares the ground for the acceptance of violent action, which finally ends up with Jihadism. An intersectional approach seems to be more productive, however, in order to better understand and explain the absence of mutual identity that we empirically observe today between fundamentalist socialization and the commitment to violence. In the today's context, Jihadism is the prerogative of actors who are radicalized as an opposition to the world and to the politics which harm them and not necessarily by a pre-existing fundamentalist ethics. Non-violent Salafism, rather, constitutes a form of religious radicalism that is a response to broader dynamics of anomy, marginalization, and globalization. Salafism, Jihadism, and radicalization certainly interact, but they do so within the framework of socio-political contexts. The careful analysis of these contexts suggests distinguishing between religious intransigence and political radicalism, and to refute the systematic nature of any links between fundamentalism and violence. The majority cases of the present-day radicalization do not occur among those who are seeking more and deeper religious practice.

REFERENCES

Adraoui, M.A. 2020. *Salafism Goes Global: From the Gulf to the French Banlieues.* New York: Oxford University Press.

Bunzel, C. 2017. Caliphate in Disarray: Theological Turmoil in the Islamic State. *Jihadica*, October 3 [Online]. Available at http://www.jihadica.com/caliphate-in-disarray/. Accessed 4 October 2021.

Filiu, J.P. 2012. *Apocalypse in Islam.* Berkeley, CA: University of California Press.

Gerges, F.A. 2017. *ISIS: A History.* Princeton, NJ: Princeton University Press.

Khosrokhavar, F. 2021. *Jihadism in Europe: European Youth and the New Caliphate.* New York, NY: Oxford University Press.

Roy, O. 2017. *Jihad and Death: The Global Appeal of the Islamic State.* New York, NY: Oxford University Press.

Weber, M. 1993. *The Sociology of Religion.* Boston: Beacon Press.

Wiktorowicz, Q. 2006. Anatomy of the Salafi Movement. *Studies in Conflict & Terrorism* 29 (3): 207–239.

CHAPTER 10

By Way of Conclusion: Salafism, a Container More Than a Content? Beyond the Essentialization of a Fundamentalism

Abstract This attempt at a conclusion asks what paths contemporary Salafism is likely to take, and whether the hypothesis of increasing political and religious fragmentation in increasingly changing contexts is plausible.

Keyword Possible evolutions for contemporary salafism

Salafism has not only imposed itself as a major religious reality in an ever increasingly globalized religious landscape but also as a central political theme. Certain analyses highlight the role of Salafism as the cause of phenomena of political and ideological violence initiated by Jihadist movements and whose impact can be felt at a worldwide level, particularly in the form of fighters operating on several continents (Latin America and the Far East being exceptions). Some other approaches perceive it as a strong factor of split with their environment for young generations in search of a total and intransigent identity, or even as a vector of growing competition with so-called traditional forms of Islam (meaning those rooted in a local or national culture). The explanation does remain the same. The doctrinal infrastructure of Salafism is said to determine a relationship to the world which passes from moral separation pushing *a minimum* to categorically condemn what is not the "true" Islam to total

© The Author(s), under exclusive license to Springer Nature Switzerland AG 2022
M.-A. Adraoui, *Understanding Salafism*, The Sciences Po Series in International Relations and Political Economy, https://doi.org/10.1007/978-3-031-18089-7_10

violence of an organization as IS. Stated otherwise, while contemporary forms of Salafism can vary as concerns in particular the relationship to politics, subversion, and the type of vehemence envisioned against the "heterodox" or non-Islamic other, it is really a question of a difference of degree and not of kind between various conceptions of this type of reform that can be observed today.

Still, if fundamentalist forms of religion all have in common supposedly overstepping history by wanting to return to the early stage of faith (otherwise stated as organizing themselves around philosophical notions of *ideal* and *origin*), Salafism can also be seen as a partially specific reformist movement. By being at once orthodox content but also methodological last rites (i.e., a way of reading and interpreting the paradigmatic sources of Islam), *al-salafiyya* actually echoes a more dynamic approach than what one might first think. The modern and contemporary history of Muslim societies thus produced multiple versions of this revivalism, which, as radically attached to the Ancients as they claim to be, lead to different conclusions in terms of philosophical and political orientation, are not any less based on the same assumed mental topography as the branches studied here. This is the case of the modernist Salafism at the end of the nineteenth century, as viscerally anticolonial as it turned out to be was intellectually open to other influences. Moreover, any integralist and radical construction of religion evolves while redefining its radicalism in relation to its desire to have an impact on the rest of the social body, as shown by the switch to the organized activism of certain Salafist branches (some representatives of which, as much by interest as by sociological change, admit to reformulating a part of their initial credo in the image of certain movements coming from the Muslim Brotherhood experience before them, for instance). The Salafist matrix thus drives through major changes, due to historical contingencies, opposed and even contradictory imaginaries, making it impossible to evoke it in an unequivocal way today. Because it is first a religious container that has progressively become ideological content, it is difficult to want to anticipate the future of this reformism. The diversity of socio-cultural contexts in which it will increasingly be a part as well as the fear of anarchy (in quietist forms), the call of politics (among participationists), or the one of violence (for Jihadists) in environments within which Islam provides both the language of rebellion and of resignation (thus making any culturalist judgment null and void) makes it effectively impossible to apprehend in a singular way. As a result, wanting to understand Salafism seems to make it more than ever necessary to focus on disparate and interactive factors that explain—yesterday, today, and tomorrow—phenomena of ideologization of faith and the desire to call a past era as a witness against the torments of a despised present time.

By virtue of all these factors, if one can venture many hypotheses for the future of Salafism, that of its increasing fragmentation or even its overcoming seems plausible. In fact, it is possible to envisage less radical ideological content over the next few decades, making Salafism a social and religious conservatism, but without any pretention to completely transform society and the political field. Other religious traditions, such as Christianity and Judaism, have in fact led over the centuries to religiously conservative ethics without ever generating a political revolution, as can be seen in Mormonism in the United States or in the *Habad Lubavitch* movement in many European countries. On the other hand, the violent currents, as we have tried to highlight, are characterized sociologically by a dynamic of decoupling from a puritanical Salafist socialization, the central question here becoming what can happen to Jihadism if its members see in it today and even more so in the future an ethic of violence to the detriment of an increasingly secondary religious rigorism. Finally, in the institutional political field, what can happen to groups and parties that depend on closed political systems in many Arab countries, for example, or that are simply in the process of disintegrating, as can be observed in failed states such as Syria, Libya, or Yemen? In this respect, the inexistence of perennial political structures in many national contexts, which have moreover oscillated in the Arab world for several decades between sociological modernization and fundamentalist temptation, prevents us from believing in the imminence of a generalized Salafist revolution, even though its cultural codes are in some places there to suggest the contrary.

References

Aarts, P., and C. Roelants. 2015. *Saudi Arabia. A Kingdom in Peril.* New York, NY: Oxford University Press.
Abbas, A., and F. Griffel, eds. 2007. *Shari'a: Islamic Law in the Contemporary Context.* Stanford, CA: Stanford University Press.
Abbas, T. 2019. *Islamophobia and Radicalisation: A Vicious Cycle.* Oxford: Oxford University Press.
Abbas, T. 2021. *Countering Violent Extremism: The International Deradicalization Agenda.* London: I.B. Tauris.
Abou El Fadl, K. 1999. The Rules of Killing at War: An Inquiry into Classical Sources. *The Muslim World* 89 (2): 155–157.
Abou El Fadl, K. 2001. *Rebellion and Violence in Islamic Law.* Cambridge: Cambridge University Press.
Adraoui, M.A. 2020. *Salafism Goes Global: From the Gulf to the French Banlieues.* New York: Oxford University Press.
Afsaruddin, A. 2022. *Jihad: What Everyone Wants to Know.* New York, NY: Oxford University Press.
Ahmad, A. 2017. *Jihad&Co.: Black Markets and Islamist Power.* New York, NY: Oxford University Press.
Al-Fawzān, S. 1990. *Al-walā' wa al-barā'.* JIMAS.
Alimi, E.Y., C. Demetriou, and L. Bosi. 2015. *The Dynamics of Radicalization: A Relational and Comparative Perspective.* Oxford: Oxford University Press.
Al-Rasheed, M. 2010. *A History of Saud Arabia.* Cambridge: Cambridge University Press.

Al-Rasheed, M. 2006. *Contesting the Saudi State: Islamic Voices from a New Generation*. Cambridge: Cambridge University Press.

Al-Rasheed, M. 2016. *Muted Modernists: The Struggle over Divine Politics in Saudi Arabia*. Oxford: Oxford University Press.

Al-Rasheed, M. 2007. *Contesting the Saudi State. Islamic Voices from a New Generation*. Cambridge: Cambridge University Press.

Ashour, O. 2009. *The De-Radicalization of Jihadists: Transforming Armed Islamist Movements*. London: Routledge.

Ashour, O. 2021. *How ISIS Fights: Military Tactics in Iraq, Syria, Libya and Egypt*. Edinburgh: Edinburgh University Press.

Atran, S. 2011. *Talking to the Enemy: Violent Extremism, Sacred Values, and What It Means to Be Human*. London: Penguin Books.

Baker-Beall, Christopher, ed. 2014. *Counter-Radicalisation: Critical Perspectives*. London: Routledge.

Bano, M., ed. 2021. *Salafi Social and Political Movements: National and Transnational Contexts*. Edinburgh: Edinburgh University Press.

Binns, J. 2008. *The Christian Orthodox Churches*. Cambridge: Cambridge University Press.

Bjorgo, T., and J.G. Horgan, eds. 2009. *Leaving Terrorism Behind: Individual and Collective Disengagement*. London: Routledge.

Bonnefoy, L. 2012. *Salafism in Yemen: Transnationalism and Religious Identity*. New York: Oxford University Press.

Bonney, R. 2004. *Jihad: From Qur'an to Bin Laden*. Basingstoke: Palgrave Macmillan.

Brachman, J.M. 2008. *Global Jihadism: Theory and Practice*. London: Routledge.

Braddock, K. 2020. *Weaponized Words*. Cambridge: Cambridge University Press.

Bradley, J.R. 2005. *Saudi Arabia Exposed. Inside a Kingdom in Crisis*. Basingstoke: Palgrave Macmillan.

Bunzel, C. 2017. Caliphate in Disarray: Theological Turmoil in the Islamic State. *Jihadica*, October 3 [Online]. Available at http://www.jihadica.com/caliphate-in-disarray/. Accessed 4 October 2021.

Burgat, F. 2019. *Understanding Political Islam*. Manchester: Manchester University Press.

Byman, D. 2015. *Al Qaeda, The Islamic State and the Global Jihadist Movement: What Everyone Needs to Know*. New York, NY: Oxford University Press.

Byman, D. 2019. *Road Warriors: Foreign Fighters in the Armies of Jihad*. New York, NY: Oxford University Press.

Calvert, J. 2010. *Sayyid Qutb and the Origins of Radical Islamism*. New York, NY: Columbia University Press.

Cavatorta, F., and F. Merone, eds. 2017. *Salafism after the Arab Awakening: Contending with People's Power*. New York, NY: Oxford University Press.

Coleman, John. 1992. Catholic Integralism as a Fundamentalism. In *Fundamentalism in Comparative Perspective*, ed. Lawrence Kaplan, 74–95. Amherst, MA: University of Massachusetts Press.
Commins, D. 2006. *The Wahhabi Mission and Saudi Arabia*. New York, NY: I.B. Tauris.
Cook, D. 2005. *Understanding Jihad*. Berkeley, CA: University of California Press.
Coolsaet, Rik, ed. 2016. *Jihadi Terrorism and the Radicalisation Challenge: European and American Experiences*. London: Routledge.
Court, J.M. 2008. *Approaching the Apocalypse: A Short History of Christian Millenarianism*. London: I. B. Tauris.
Crenshaw, M., and J. Pimlott. 2019. *Encyclopedia of World Terrorism*. London: Routledge.
Crone, P. 2004. *God's Rule-Government and Islam: Six Centuries of Medieval Islamic Thought*. New York, NY: Columbia University Press.
Delong Bas, N. 2004. *Wahhabi Islam: From Revival and Reform to Global Jihad*. New York, NY: Oxford University Press.
Demichelis, M. 2021. *Violence in Early Islam: Religious Narratives, the Arab Conquests and the Canonization of Jihad*. London: I.B. Tauris.
Donegani, J.M. 1993. *La liberté de choisir: Pluralisme religieux et pluralisme politique dans le catholicisme français contemporain*. Paris: Presses de la FNSP.
Doyle, N.J., and I. Ahmad, eds. 2018. *(Il)liberal Europe: Islamophobia, Modernity and Radicalization*. London: Routledge.
Egerton, F. 2011. *Jihad in the West: The Rise of Militant Islam*. Cambridge: Cambridge University Press.
Esposito, J., ed. 2003a. *The Oxford Dictionary of Islam*. New York, NY: Oxford University Press.
Esposito, J. 2003b. *Unholy War: Terror in the Name of Islam*. New York, NY: Oxford University Press.
Fadil, N., and F. Ragazzi, eds. 2019. *Jihadi Terrorism and the Radicalization Challenge in Europe*. London: I.B. Tauris.
Fadil, N., F. Ragazzi, and M. De Koning. 2019. *Radicalization in Belgium and the Netherlands: Critical Perspectives on Violence and Security*. London: I.B. Tauris.
Farquhar, M. 2016. *Circuits of Faith: Migration, Education and the Wahhabi Mission*. Stanford, CA: Stanford University Press.
Filiu, J.P. 2012. *Apocalypse in Islam*. Berkeley, CA: University of California Press.
Filiu, J.P. 2015. *From Deep State to Islamic State: The Arab Counter-Revolution and its Jihadi Legacy*. New York, NY: Oxford University Press.
Foucault, M. 2012. *The Order of Things: An Archeology of the Human Sciences*. New York: Vintage.

Gambetta, D., and S. Hertog. 2016. *Engineers of Jihad: The Curious Connection Between Violent Extremism and Education*. Princeton, NJ: Princeton University Press.
Gerges, F.A. 2006. *Journey of the Jihadist*. Harcourt.
Gerges, F.A. 2009. *The Far Enemy: Why Jihad Went Global*. Cambridge: Cambridge University Press.
Gerges, F.A. 2011. *The Rise and Fall of Al-Qaeda*. Oxford: Oxford University Press.
Gerges, F.A. 2017. *ISIS: A History*. Princeton, NJ: Princeton University Press.
Hamdeh, E. 2021. *Salafism and Traditionalism: Scholarly Authority in Modern Islam*. Cambridge: Cambridge University Press.
Hasaan, N. 2006. *Laskar Jihad: Islam, Militancy and the Quest for Identity in Post-New Order in Indonesia*. Ithaca, NY: Cornell University Press.
Hashim, A.S. 2017. *The Caliphate at War: The Ideological, Organizational and Military Innovations of Islamic State*. Oxford: Oxford University Press.
Hashmi, S.S., ed. 2002. *Islamic Political Ethics: Civil Society, Pluralism, and Conflict*. Princeton, NJ: Princeton University Press.
Hatina, M. 2012. Redeeming Sunni Islam: Al-Qaida's Polemic Against the Muslim Brothers. *British Journal of Middle East Studies* 39 (1): 101–113.
Haykel, B. 2003. *Revival and Reform in Islam: The Legacy of Muhammad Al-Shawkani*. Cambridge: Cambridge University Press.
Haykel, B., and A. Al-Shihabi. 2016. *The Saudi Kingdom: Between the Jihadi Hammer and the Iranian Anvil*. Markus Wiener Publishers.
Hegghammer, T. 2010. *Jihad in Saudi Arabia. Violence and Pan-Islamism Since 1979*. Cambridge: Cambridge University Press.
Hegghammer, T. 2017. *Jihadi Culture: The Art and Social Practices of Militant Islamists*. Cambridge: Cambridge University Press.
Hegghammer, T., and S. Lacroix. 2011. *The Meccan Rebellion: The Story of Juhayman al-'Utaybi Revisited*. Amal Press.
Hoffman, B., and F. Reinares, eds. 2014. *The Evolution of the Global Terrorist Threat: From 9/11 to Osama Bin Laden's Death*. New York, NY: Columbia University Press.
Hoffman, B. 2017. *Inside Terrorism*. New York, NY: Columbia University Press.
Holbrook, D. 2014. *The Al-Qaeda Doctrine: The Framing and Evolution of the Leadership's Public Discourse*. London: Bloomsbury Academic.
Horgan, J.G. 2002. *The Psychology of Terrorism*. London: Routledge.
Hoyland, R. 2014. *In God's Path: The Arab Conquests and the Creation of an Islamic Empire*. Oxford: Oxford University Press.
Ibrahim, R. 2007. *The Al Qaeda Reader: The Essential Texts of Osama Bin Laden's Terrorist Organization*. New York: Broadway Books.
Inge, A. 2016. *The Making of a Muslim Salafi Woman*. Oxford: Oxford University Press.

Ingram, H.J., C. Whiteside, and C. Winter. 2020. *The ISIS Reader: Milestone Texts of the Islamic State Movement*. Oxford: Oxford University Press.
Ismail, R. 2021. *Rethinking Salafism: The Transnational Networks of Salafi 'Ulama in Egypt, Kuwait, and Saudi Arabia*. New York, NY: Oxford University Press.
Joffe, G., ed. 2012. *Islamist Radicalisation in North Africa: Politics and Process*. London: Routledge.
Jones, C., and R. Narag. 2016. *Inmate Radicalisation and Recruitment in Prisons*. London: Routledge.
Juergensmeyer, M. 2003. *Terror in the Mind of God: The Global Rise of Religious Violence*. Berkeley, CA: University of California Press.
Juergensmeyer, M., M. Kitts, and M. Jerryson, eds. 2015. *The Oxford Handbook of Religion and Violence*. Oxford: Oxford University Press.
Kepel, G. 2003a. *Jihad: The Trail of Political Islam*. Cambridge, MA: Harvard University Press.
Kepel, G. 2003b. *Muslim Extremism in Egypt: The Prophet and Pharaoh*. Berkeley, CA: University of California Press.
Kepel, G., and J.-P. Milelli, eds. 2010. *Al Qaeda in Its Own Words*. Cambridge, MA: Harvard University Press.
Kepel, G. 2017. *Terror in France: The Rise of Jihad in the West*. Princeton, NJ: Princeton University Press.
Kerr, M.H. 1972. *The Arab Cold War: Gamal 'Abd-Al Nasir and His Rivals, 1958–1970*. Oxford: Oxford University Press.
Khadduri, M. 1955. *War and Peace in the Law of Islam*. Baltimore, MD: Johns Hopkins University Press.
Khalil, M.H. 2013a. *Islam and the Fate of Others: The Salvation Question*, 2013. Oxford: Oxford University Press.
Khalil, M.H. 2013b. *Between Heaven and Hell: Islam, Salvation, and the Fate of Others*. Oxford: Oxford University Press.
Khosrokhavar, F. 2017. *Radicalization: Why Some People Choose the Path of Violence*. New York: The New Press.
Khosrokhavar, F. 2021. *Jihadism in Europe: European Youth and the New Caliphate*. New York, NY: Oxford University Press.
Klause, J. 2021. *Jihadism in the West: A Thirty Tear History*. Oxford: Oxford University Press.
Kruglanski, A.W., J.J. Bélanger, and R. Gunaratna. 2019. *The Three Pillars of Radicalization: Needs, Narratives and Networks*. Oxford: Oxford University Press.
Kundnani, A. 2012. Radicalization: The Journey of a Concept. *Race and Class* 54 (2): 3–25.
Lacroix, S. 2011. *Awakening Islam. The Politics of Religious Dissent in Contemporary Saudi Arabia*. Cambridge, MA: Harvard University Press.

Lauzière, H. 2015. *The Making of Salafism: Islamic Reform in the Twentieth Century*. New York, NY: Columbia University Press.
Li, D. 2019. *The Universal Enemy: Jihad, Empire and the Challenge of Solidarity*. Stanford, CA: Stanford University Press.
Lia, B. 1999. *The Society of the Muslim Brothers in Egypt: The Rise of an Islamic Mass Movement*. Reading: Ithaca Press.
Lia, B. 2016. Jihadism in the Arab World After 2011: Explaining its Expansion. *Middle East Policy* 23 (4): 74–91.
Lister, C. 2016. *The Syrian Jihad: Al-Qaeda, the Islamic State and the Evolution of an Insurgency*. New York, NY: Oxford University Press.
Mandaville, P. 2020. *Islam and Politics*. London: Routledge.
Manne, R. 2017. *The Mind of the Islamic State: ISIS and the Ideology of the Caliphate*. Amherst: Prometheus Books.
Martinez, L. 2000. *The Algerian Civil War: 1990–1998*. New York, NY: Columbia University Press.
McCants, W. 2015a. *The ISIS Apocalypse: The History, Strategy, and Doomsday Vision of the Islamic State*. New York: St Martin's Press.
McCants, W. 2015b. *The Believer: How an Introvert with a Passion for Religion and Soccer Became Abu Bakr Al-Baghdadi, Leader of the Islamic State*. Washington, DC: Brookings Institution Press.
Meijer, R., ed. 2009. *Global Salafism: Islam's New Religious Movement*. New York, NY: Oxford University Press.
Melchert, C. 2006. *Makers of the Muslim World: Ahmad Ibn Hanbal*. Oxford: Oneworld.
Meleagrou-Hitchens, A. 2020. *Incitement: Anwar Al-Awlaki's Western Jihad*. Cambridge, MA: Harvard University Press.
Moskalenko, S., and C. McCauley. 2020. *Radicalization to Terrorism: What Everyone Needs to Know*. Oxford: Oxford University Press.
Mouline, N. 2014. *The Clerics of Islam: Religious Authority and Political Power in Saudi Arabia*. New Haven, CT: Yale University Press.
Mouline, N. 2016. *Le Califat. Histoire politique de l'islam*. Paris: Flammarion.
Nesser, P. 2018. *Islamist Terrorism in Europe*. Oxford: Oxford University Press.
Neumann, P.R., ed. 2015. *Radicalization*. London: Routledge.
Neumann, P.R. 2016. *Radicalized: New Jihadists and the Threat to the West*. London: I.B. Tauris.
Olsson, S. 2016. *Contemporary Puritan Salafism: A Swedish Case Study*. Sheffield: Equinox.
Ould Mohamedou, M.M. 2011. *Understanding Al Qaeda: Changing War and Global Politics*. London: Pluto Press.
Ould Mohamedou, M.M. 2018. *A Theory of ISIS: Political Violence and the Transformation of the Global Order*. Chicago, IL: University of Chicago Press.

Pall, Z. 2018. *Salafism in Lebanon: Local and Transnational Movements.* Cambridge: Cambridge University Press.
Parker, T., and N. Sitter. 2016. The Four Horsemen of Terrorism. It's Not Waves, It's Strains. *Terrorism and Political Violence* 28 (2): 197–216.
Peters, R. 1996. *Jihad in Classical and Modern Islam: A Reader.* Princeton, NJ: Markus Wiener Publishers.
Piscatori, J. 1991. *Islamic Fundamentalism and the Gulf Crisis.* Chicago, IL: American Academy of Arts and Sciences, Fundamentalism Project.
Poulat, E. 1986. *L'Église, c'est un monde: L'ecclésiosphère.* Paris: Éditions du Cerf.
Rabasa, A., and C. Benard. 2014. *Eurojihad: Patterns of Islamist Radicalization and Terrorism in Europe.* Cambridge: Cambridge University Press.
Ranstorp, M., ed. 2010. *Understanding Violent Radicalisation: Terrorist and Jihadist Movements in Europe.* London: Routledge.
Rapaport, Y., and S. Ahmed. 2015. *Ibn Taymiyya and His Times.* New York: Oxford University Press.
Rapoport, D.C. 2001. The Fourth Wave: September 11 and the History of Terrorism. *Current History* 100 (650): 419–424.
Rock-Singer, A. 2022. *In the Shade of the Sunna: Salafi Piety in the Twentieth Century Middle East.* Berkeley: University of California Press.
Rosenwein, B.H. 2006. *Emotional Communities in the Early Middle Ages.* Ithaca, NY: Cornell University Press.
Roy, O. 1994. *The Failure of Political Islam*, 199. Cambridge, MA: Harvard University Press.
Roy, O. 2004. *Globalized Islam: The Search for a New Umma.* New York, NY: Columbia University Press.
Roy, O. 2014. *The Holy Ignorance: When Religion and Culture Part Ways.* New York, NY: Columbia University Press.
Roy, O. 2017. *Jihad and Death: The Global Appeal of the Islamic State.* New York, NY: Oxford University Press.
Sageman, M. 2004. *Understanding Terror Networks.* Philadelphia, PA: University of Pennsylvania Press.
Sageman, M. 2011. *Leaderless Jihad: Terror Networks in the Twenty-First Century.* Philadelphia, PA: University of Pennsylvania Press.
Sageman, M. 2016. *Misunderstanding Terrorism.* Philadelphia, PA: University of Pennsylvania Press.
Sageman, M. 2017. *Turning to Political Violence: The Emergence of Terrorism.* Philadelphia, PA: University of Pennsylvania Press.
Scheuer, M. 2003. *Through Our Enemies' Eyes.* Washington, DC: Potomac Books.
Schmitt, C. 2007. *The Concept of the Political.* Chicago, IL: University of Chicago Press.

Günther, S., and L. Todd (eds.). 2016. *Roads to Paradise: Eschatology and Concepts of the Hereafter in Islam* (2 Vols.). Leiden: Brill.

Shoemaker, S.J. 2018. *The Apocalypse of Empire: Imperial Eschatology in Late Antiquity and Early Islam.* Philadelphia, PA: University of Pennsylvania Press.

Sluglett, P., ed. 2019. *Violent Radical Movements in the Arab World: The Ideology and Politics of Non-State Actors.* London: I.B. Tauris.

Staffel, S., and A. Awan, eds. 2016. *Jihadism Transformed: Al-Qaeda and Islamic State's Global Battle of Ideas.* Oxford: Oxford University Press.

Steinberg, G. 2013. *German Jihad: On the Internationalization of Islamist Terrorism.* New York, NY: Columbia University Press.

Svensson, I. 2012. *Ending Holy Wars: Religion and Conflict Resolution in Civil Wars.* Brisbane: University of Queensland Press.

Thomas, D. 2016. *Générations djihadistes. Al-Qaïda – État islamique: Histoire d'une lutte fratricide.* Paris: Michalon.

Thurston, A. 2018. *Salafism in Nigeria: Islam, Preaching and Politics.* Cambridge: Cambridge University Press.

Thurston, A. 2020. *Jihadists of North Africa and the Sahel: Local Politics and Rebel Groups.* Cambridge: Cambridge University Press.

Turner, J.A. 2014. *Religious Ideology and the Roots of the Global Jihad.* Basingstoke: Palgrave Macmillan.

Wagemakers, J. 2012a. The Enduring Legacy of the Second Saudi State: Quietist and Radical Wahhabi Contestations of *Al-Wala' wal-Bara'*. *International Journal of Middle East Studies* 44 (1): 93–110.

Wagemakers, J. 2012b. *A Quietist Jihadi: The Ideology and Influence of Abu Muhammad Al-Maqdisi.* Cambridge: Cambridge University Press.

Wagemakers, J. 2016. *Salafism in Jordan: Political Islam in a Quietist Community.* Cambridge: Cambridge University Press.

Walls, J.L., ed. 2008. *The Oxford Handbook of Eschatology.* Oxford: Oxford University Press.

Wasserstein, D.J. 2017. *Black Banners of ISIS: The Roots of the New Caliphate.* New Haven, CT: Yale University Press.

Weber, E. 2000. *Apocalypses: Prophecies, Cults, and Millennial Beliefs through the Ages.* Cambridge, MA: Harvard University Press.

Weber, M. 1993. *The Sociology of Religion.* Boston: Beacon Press.

Weber, M. 2004. *The Protestant Ethic and the "Spirit" of Capitalism.* New York: Penguin Books.

Wehrey, F., and A. Boukhars. 2019. *Salafism in the Maghreb: Politics, Piety, and Militancy.* Oxford: Oxford University Press.

Wiktorowicz, Q. 2001. The New Global Threat: Transnational Salafis and Jihad. *Middle East Policy* 8 (4): 18–38.

Wiktorowicz, Q. 2005a. A Genealogy of Radical Islam. *Studies in Conflict and Terrorism* 28 (2): 75–97.

Wiktorowicz, Q. 2005b. *Radical Islam Rising: Muslim Extremism in the West*. Rowman & Littlefield Publishers.

Wiktorowicz, Q. 2006. Anatomy of the Salafi Movement. *Studies in Conflict & Terrorism* 29 (3): 207–239.

Zelin, A.Y. 2020. *Your Sons Are at Your Service: Tunisia's Missionaries of Jihad*. New York, NY: Columbia University Press.

GPSR Compliance
The European Union's (EU) General Product Safety Regulation (GPSR) is a set of rules that requires consumer products to be safe and our obligations to ensure this.

If you have any concerns about our products, you can contact us on

ProductSafety@springernature.com

In case Publisher is established outside the EU, the EU authorized representative is:

Springer Nature Customer Service Center GmbH
Europaplatz 3
69115 Heidelberg, Germany

www.ingramcontent.com/pod-product-compliance
Ingram Content Group UK Ltd.
Pitfield, Milton Keynes, MK11 3LW, UK
UKHW021251180426
11946UKWH00004B/85